LAST MAN

David W. Neil

Z. Neil

With Grateful Thanks

LAST MAN STANDING

Chuck one up!

Born in Wallsend in 1929, Dave Neil has lived nothing short of a colourful life. Having done everything from serving his country during the tragedies of the Malayan Emergency to running his own dancing club alongside his wife Betty to raising and sustaining a family amongst it all, he has now decided to put pen to paper and turn to writing.

Alongside this long-form publication, Dave has also published a series of heartfelt poetry anthologies recounting his life of equal parts love and loss.

Praise for the novel

I am greatly impressed with this manuscript for many reasons.

First: it is a combination of personal recollections and of a family story both of which are intertwined and interlocking, and so far-ranging.

Secondly: it will appeal to social historians as well as those with a particular interest in the military life and it gives a realistic remembrance to those who have seen service and known the value of comradeship.

Thirdly: and what makes it so unique, it is not written in the normal style of memoirs, which tend to brush over the difficult bits and fill out the good bits. This is just 'how it happened'.

Fourthly: it is absolutely honest and straight and thus is very much a portrait of the man I have grown to know over a number of years, and whose decency, integrity and modesty flow through the story.

I read the words and can hear him talking as he writes: a good story in so many ways.

General Sir Garry Johnson, KCB, OBE, MC

LAST MAN STANDING

A remarkable book written by a 93-year-old former soldier after a memory gap of 70 plus years, giving the reader a real impression of being there with him.

The author's recollections are clearly recorded with detailed descriptions of places by name and of incidents. So many of the places mentioned are well known to me, the transit camp at Nee Soon, Seremban where we had our RHQ, Kuantan where we went on holiday in 1978, the Cameron Highlands where I spent five months in that little camp with a deserted bungalow which we were told had been "burnt down by the 4th Hussars".

He correctly queries why this period in the history of Malaysia was termed 'an emergency' when it accounted for the lives of so many civilians and military personnel.

It was a great tribute to the author that he was elected chairman of the National Malaya and Borneo Veterans Association which triggered his several trips with his wife back to the area since the end of his services.

Anthony Gibson (formerly Honorary Colonel, Northumberland Hussars)

David Neil's aptly titled autobiography of his 90+ years is wide-ranging and written in his own inimitable style. It is the story of a proud Geordie lad's journey – so far – through a full and varied life. It is a love story, and it is a chronicle of human interaction.

David covers his early life, good memories

of summer holidays staying with an aunt in Kent, enemy action over Tyneside, early work experiences, then into the Army which has been such a significant factor for him.

Very understandably, his memories of four years in Malaya fighting Communist insurgents are vivid, as is his anger that those who fought there, and even more so those who died, many of them National Servicemen, have had at best rather grudging Government recognition. He tells of lining the ship's side with comrades, homeward bound, looking shorewards to where those not returning lay buried and all saying, 'Sleep well, bonnie lads'.

He goes on to describe life as a trucker, with its own comradeship, and his very considerable involvement in the local and National Malaya & Borneo Veterans Association, rising to National Chairman.

David's family life is clearly very important to him. We learn of his marriage to Betty, their life together, the birth of David junior and Fiona, his and Betty's involvement in dancing, the sadness of Betty's and Fiona's deaths. Holidays in Malaya, years after his soldiering there, have built up a great affection for that country and its people. David could have had a second home there, but tells how his heart is on Tyneside, where he wishes to end his days.

David mentions no names, to spare any embarrassment. He sticks to that, save by consent, his family and his loyal and hard-working secretary Valerie Nisbet, who has transcribed David's longhand and deserves much thanks.

LAST MAN STANDING

He quotes the old soldiers' phrase 'Don't join if you can't take a joke'. Describing himself as now waiting in the Departure Lounge, he instructs his son when the time comes to spare no expense and 'get two bags of crisps'. One has the feeling that David will receive much more than that – he certainly deserves it.

Revd. Timothy Duff

I found David's book really interesting.

In it, he goes through many changes in his varied life. Some humorous, some happy and some really tragic and very sad times! All of which he has shouldered with strength and fortitude.

A good read!

Brenda Dudding

I thoroughly enjoyed reading David's account of his long and eventful life. He tells his story with both wit and complete honesty and his most poignant recollections will bring tears to the eyes of any reader.

David recollects his experiences with just enough detail for the reader to feel the emotion of each memory, whether it is happy or sad.

In the same way, we get some insight into the relationship he' has enjoyed with family, friends, brothers in arms and the many colleagues he tells us about. Again, there is always just enough detail for us to understand the relevance of each person in David's amazing life and why they feature in his story.

Moreover, his wicked sense of humour is never far away in any situation.

There is nothing that comes across stronger than his eternal love for his amazing wife Betty. It is clear that they had the strongest love, which still endures, for David. He came across as a proud family man through and through an it is truly heartening.

However, it is the account of his years in the Army, and especially his time in the Far East, that is most astounding. David down-plays the life-threatening situations he and his comrades faced, but he still creates a sense of the real danger all around them.

His account of this time in this life is very humble and extremely interesting. We are left with the knowledge that these men, though unassuming, were very valiant throughout all that time.

It is evident that David is a very special individual and has always strove to do the very best. His dedication making a success of the NMBVA exemplifies this.

There are so many lessons for life in David's book, I feel more humble and wiser for having read it. But one thing it certainly leaves you wanting is a refreshing bottle of Tiger!

Mary Glindon, MP for North Tyneside

Dedication

For my darling Betty, and
my whole family, David,
Christine, Kate and Adam plus
my two wonderful friends
Brenda and Sharon.

LAST MAN STANDING

DAVID NEIL

Published by Request a Guest 2021

276 Whitley Road
Whitley Bay, Tyne and Wear NE26 2TG

www.requestaguest.co.uk

ISBN 978-1-914408-56-4

A CIP catalogue record for this book
is available from the British Library

This book is a work of non-fiction based on the life, experiences
and recollections of the author. In some limited cases names of
people, places, dates, sequences or the detail of events have
been altered solely to respect the privacy of others. The
author has stated to the publishers that, except in such
circumstances, the contents of this book are factually
accurate.

Typeset in Nimbus Mono by URW Type Foundry GmbH,
Hamburg, Germany

Printed and bound in Great Britain by
Biddles Books

LAST MAN STANDING

Recognising Sacrifice

This novel was published with the intention of supporting and raising money and awareness for the Gurkha Welfare Trust. The author hopes his deeply held respect for this organisation is recognised and warmly welcomed.

Foreword

When asked by the author if I would write the foreword for this book, I accepted without hesitation. It was only when I sat down to start the task that it dawned on me the challenge of doing this and doing so effectively. The point being that the author is my father, he's in his 92nd year and this is the first book he's ever written. I've never written a book, nor have I ever previously written a foreword to a book. In fact, whilst I do a lot of reading, I'm not by any means an avid reader of books.

So how did this crazy situation come about? Well, it began during the year 2020, which just about everyone on Planet Earth that year will know only too well was the year of Covid-19 pandemic and the "lockdown". It was a year that began largely like any other, but for my dad life had already started to become increasingly frustrating. He'd entered his 9th decade and although still very much as sharp as ever upstairs (i.e. – mentally), physically he was now somewhat restricted. He'd recently given up driving and getting around on his legs was a strain. He was now more housebound than ever, relying more on the company of visitors than ever before, friends and family. My mother had passed away several years earlier and we sadly lost my younger sister some years ago too. My dad was therefore at home alone. Then with the Covid-19 pandemic taking over, there could be no visitors apart my wife and myself. We in effect were acting as his carers. It really hit him hard. He's pretty good in that as well

LAST MAN STANDING

as having TV to keep him entertained, he can operate his home computer and so manage emails, YouTube and the likes. But in a lockdown, even these can only help to a certain degree. When I was visiting and checking on his welfare, my dad would often like to talk about various aspects over his life and particularly his army days. From this, I pointed out to him how one day when he's no longer with us, so many of his experiences and learning through life will be gone forever. I suggested that to help occupy his time, maybe he should begin writing down all his memories. The thought at that stage was not particularly of developing it into a book and I wouldn't even say that he was sure about doing this at first. However, before too long and clearly having given this some thought, he was off and running with the idea and well, here we are!

The writing of what has become the book, took him quite a few months. He toyed with what to include and what not and he sometimes needed to take breaks of several days or more. I could tell that occasionally when recollecting some of the stories, it was unlocking otherwise dormant and at times unpleasant memories, and this could be quite emotional for him. With coming up on 92 years of life to draw upon, I know there is quite a lot more that my dad could have included. But with the background I've explained in terms of how this has come about, there's enough included for now and it's far too early to start talking about a sequel.

He would hand write page after page, I would collect and post these to the wonderful Val who you learn a little more about from reading the book. Val typed up each page, checking and tidying it all as she went through collating the story into something that could then be sent to Mark the printer, who has also been so helpful and supportive to my dad. Once it had all been pulled together, the draft had several reviewers, one of which was myself. My role in reviewing this piece of work however, was a little different. I was reading my father's recollection of his life and for around two thirds of this, I existed in it to a greater or lesser extent. Even in the earlier chapters that cover the times before I had arrived, this has been quite intriguing for me, as whilst there are memories and tales that my dad had already told me about at some time or another, there were a few things I'd not otherwise been aware of.

I think I am as best placed as anyone to have been both a reviewer and the writer of the Foreword, given the nature of who and what it is about. It is perhaps a less than conventional go at what is an autobiography of sorts. But it is also a reflection on life events, people and surviving through decades that contained so much, in what was going on in the world around my dad.

From reading the book right through and so my dad's story (so far), it is contrasting in several ways. His time in the army in Malaya for example and bearing in mind he arrived there still a teenager, includes experiences that not many people today would otherwise be aware of, with stories ranging from general army life at the time, to daring and some downright tragic occurrence's. In how he adapted once home from

LAST MAN STANDING

Malaya and went about life in "civvy street", it could through this stage be regarded to a degree as relatively typical for many people. But what perhaps is a bit different is how despite a few setbacks, my dad with the support of my mother, never took too long to find a positive and an opportunity to make good of situations. Reading, reflecting and thinking about it as his son, it has brought to the fore to me, my dad's positivity, natural leadership instinct and his adaptability. If there's a particular message that I'd say comes from his story then it's as simple as, whatever life throws at you, don't be afraid to adapt and plough on through. From a childhood through the 30's and the Second World War, then a frontline soldier in a hostile conflict, followed by years of driving heavy trucks, to becoming a DJ and running dances with my mother, it's been a quite varied and contrasting route through life. And when an association was created for those who'd also served in the same conflict, he wasn't going to just join to be a member, he was very quickly elevated into a senior and leading position to help the association survive several challenges and to grow, to be effective and achieve its goals.

Did the generation of my parents have more drive, determination and resilience than the generation of my children? Or was my dad more a one-off of that generation? I guess you read this, think about it and make up your own mind. I suppose each reader of this piece of work needs to pick out what messages they get from it. One vitally important message that my dad has very much wanted to highlight through this book however, is in relation to the so called "Malayan Emergency". A costly conflict in terms of lives lost, but a conflict that has never been classed as a "war". My dad says his piece about this in the book and as he points out, of those who served with him in Malaya, my dad is probably now the remaining living member, the last man standing and their remaining spokesperson as such. If the message he relays in regard to this conflict was the only message that you were to take from this book, then I know that my dad would feel that it has been a project worth completing.

David Neil Jnr.

Introduction

I am not a writer of stories and freely admit at not being prolific in putting pen to paper. But I have undertaken this endeavour to, as I'll put it, appease my family and friends. It tells about my life and the experiences of my 90+ years.

I served in khaki uniform for twenty of those years, almost four of them in the Malaysian Emergency. During this time, I was ambushed three times and on one occasion left with life threatening injuries, having to be air lifted to BMH Singapore where he was a patient for 13 weeks, before being returned to action with his very special unit.

It must be understood this is not a diary but more a chronicle of events which had either an elevating or depressing effect on my everyday life.

I guess it also reveals me as a rather unashamed romantic, which I'll proudly admit, but I was never a flirt.

To avoid possible embarrassment or upset, I am by and large avoiding the stating people's names in the stories and events I describe here. The exceptions to this are where I have been given permission, or in some cases I've used shortened or nicknames.

CHAPTER 1

In the Beginning

After some well-intended cajoling and encouragement from my Association President, Branch Secretary, my son and family, to pen a book chronicling some of the events that I recall having occurred during my lifetime, here it is. The idea was to portray it as a story built around a chronicle of real events that involved a young soldier and his girlfriend. It guides you through their deep love for each other, how it endured some four years of separation but never faltered in all that time when I was on the other side of the world, much of the time engaged in combat. I must confess this is done with a minimum of enthusiasm, for I feel it is almost like writing my own obituary. The only consolation I can obtain is, if I take an early departure, one of those buggers can finish it off. Therefore:

In the beginning, at the GB Hunter Memorial Hospital (The Green) Wallsend, to Mr & Mrs Alfred & Ethel Neil on 22nd July 1929, a boy was born. Mother and baby were in good health. Shortly after the little boy was christened David William. So, this is the beginning of a journey that was to last 90+ years. But who knows, I am still here. You may wonder how this has happened, I must confess, I do, so please read on.

At quite an early age, I think I would be

about three years old; I burned my right hand in an accident at home. This resulted in my being rushed to hospital in Newcastle's Royal Victoria Infirmary. Sad to say and worryingly, I lapsed into septicaemia and was in a life-threatening condition for quite some time. Fortunately, my aunty was a nurse and was permitted to look after me and thanks to her care and expertise along with that of the doctors and nurses, I survived. One must think, for all this to happen so early in life, had I been born under a lucky star? You will have to wait and see.

When I had fully recovered it was time to start school, which would be at Wallsend Central Infants. I well recall my teacher was a very sweet young lady called Miss Tinkler, who I realised had the ability to keep her pupils' attention in class. I well remember on one occasion she gave us all six strips of yellow paper about 6'' x 1/2'' and asked us to arrange them into a shape we were able to think up. We all began to think and work. After a while she came around each of us. It appeared that I was the only one who hadn't made a windmill. I think there had been a considerable amount of copying, or perhaps this was an early sign of my independent nature, for I had designed a five-bar gate, and Miss told me I was artistic (teacher's pet).

The home that my parents and I lived in, was an upstairs flat, three rooms, in Laurel Street Wallsend. As there were only two bedrooms my mother and father slept in one and my mother's younger brother and I in the other.

Things began to change, as I thought, for the better. A friend of my mother's owned a shop on the Coast Road which had a big very nice flat above and so we moved in. I had my own room and a different school, the Wallsend Buddle. I also began to make new friends. My mother was expecting a baby and it was the start of the long summer school holidays. I was therefore dispatched to stay with my lovely funny aunty in Kent for the whole of that summer. The strange thing is, I always remember it as being wall to wall sunshine. I'm sure there must have been some rain. These were the happiest days of my childhood, playing in the river, picnics and fruit picking. I wished they would never end, but sad to say they inevitably do. So, I returned to my new home in Wallsend and a baby sister.

By this time my father had returned to full employment, having had to cope with three years of being unemployed off the back of what in history we know as the Great Depression. This meant that we were able to move again, this time into a brand-new self-contained home. Sadly however, the clouds of war were beginning to loom large and threatening. This didn't create an air of confidence or comfort. It rather took the shine off things for my parents, new baby and new house, with the prospect of another war. They had already lived through one.

I was getting used to my new school, my parents were busy arranging things in our new home and mum had left an old and trusted friend I called Granny Kelly, to look after the baby at her home. I was playing in the garden.

LAST MAN STANDING

I think everyone had their radios tuned in for the prime minister's speech, about 11am. I heard him announce that we were at war with Germany. No sooner had he made that declaration than the air-raid siren sounded. My mother told me to collect the baby in her pram from Granny Kelly's and run like the wind. That was about a mile distance, but I think I did it in record time, feeling like some sort of hero, only to be informed the warning was a trial and not the real thing. I think that was the first occasion I felt like a fallen idol. Oh my god, I have just realised, I am still waiting for that elusive award.

This was 1939 and ahead of us lay six years of uncertainty, shortages, air attacks, rationing and at one stage, the possibility of invasion. There was also the disruption to family lives, as many fathers and sons were called to arms.

At the beginning of this period all the schools were closed. Then after two or three months the seniors, which included my age group, were informed to attend for 2 hours a day. It was during this time when, on a very frosty foggy morning, a mixed group of girls and boys were walking to school for our 2-hour stint. Suddenly without any warning, an enemy aircraft just visible in the fog began to strafe the road we were about to cross. I think the wonderful thing about this was nobody panicked. When it had passed, we gathered together, girls and boys, to decide what to do and I clearly recall the consensus of opinion appeared to be "well if they are going to be like that we will just go home". Spirits were high and I thought they will never break us down.

So, it was on that cold foggy morning we had our first experience of being at war. There were other incidents over the following few years but in many ways and compared to other north east areas, we didn't do too badly. On one occasion during a night-time air-raid an enemy aircraft jettisoned a stick of five bombs about 300 meters from our house, one of which did not go off. The civil defence wardens and police evacuated the houses they thought could be at risk. The bomb went off at 5am and frighteningly it was only about a yard away from the path they had used to carry out the evacuation. To bring this tale to a happy ending however, when it went off a large lump of earth flew over the houses into the adjoining street, knocking an unfortunate policeman's helmet off (he was uninjured, but not amused).

By this time school had returned to normal working hours. I and my two friends decided to join the sea cadets and it was then I learnt that the civil defence were looking for young volunteers who had a bicycle. This was to fill the role of messengers if there was a breakdown in communications in an emergency. I did not respond immediately as I was about to leave school and was not sure if my future employer would approve. Shortly after, I began work in the shipyard and both my employer and my father approved. I was quite pleased with myself, could that be an early sign of a budding spirit of adventure.

LAST MAN STANDING

By this stage of the war the tide was turning in our favour, but there was still a long way to go. As for my job it was just a case of fetch and carry but did give me the opportunity to visit some of the vessels that were nearing completion, which at that age was both interesting and exciting. At that time there was an aircraft carrier, a cruiser and two destroyers which were the first of the new Battle Class. On the subject of destroyers and the war, I recall my father hurrying home to take me down to the river to see Lord Louis Mountbatten on the bridge of his renowned destroyer, HMS Kelly. This was under his orders to return to the Tyne when it had been hit by a mine and was under tow for ninety-two hours. A wonderful sight to see, for the banks of the Tyne were lined with cheering crowds of shipyard workers and the local population. The sad footnote to this gallant incident came later in the day when news was released of the large number of seamen's bodies that had been recovered from the wreckage of the ship's engine room. Their graves and memorial are in the local cemetery in the town of Hebburn on Tyne, lovingly cared for by the local council and community. Long may that continue.

In 1946 I left the shipyard at the insistence of my mother, to go and lodge away from home to work and learn a trade under her brother, who I learned to dislike in record time. Result, he attempted to humiliate me in front of my workmates which was the last straw and I was left with little choice but to, as they say, deck him and walk off the job. It was at this point I feel I broke free but shall not elaborate any further on this, as such.

7

CHAPTER 2

For King and Country

The year was 1947 and, in the August, I enlisted in the army. First, at number 5 PTC Newcastle, to begin my six weeks basic training. It wasn't too bad for I had been taught the rudiments of drill in the cadets. After the six weeks we took part in a passing out parade which was followed by a posting to RAC training regiment, the 8th Royal Tanks. My friend and I caught the train from Richmond into Darlington for a Saturday night out looking for the local dance hall and called into a pub for a pint before going on the pull. I just could not believe my eyes for there at the far end of the bar was that uncle I so disliked. The smarmy rotter was chatting up the barmaid. He was so totally engrossed in his pursuit of passion; he had not seen me. I asked my pal Tom if I wrote out a short note would he go and hand it to him. I quickly got a bit of toilet paper and wrote on it 'would you accept a pint from your nephew' and sent it to him. With an eye on the smug look on his stupid face, I had been served his pint and took it round to him. He was telling the barmaid and all and sundry "all was now forgiven". Not so, as I poured it over his stupid arrogant head. Tom and I left to applause.

Our training camp was at Catterick, as I was being trained as a driver and AFV gunner.

LAST MAN STANDING

The driving part passed; it was now time for the gunnery test. This took place at the range at Warcop in the Pennines. If the reader would pause and think this was 1947 one of the worst winters on record. Result, very little gunnery and a hell of a lot of snow clearing and helping to keep the traffic moving and digging out a farmer who wouldn't even make us a cup of tea. In the end the gunnery test was postponed indefinitely. I am still waiting, but my trigger finger is locked with arthritis so don't stand too close.

On our return to Catterick it was time to learn what our posting would be. At that time if you enlisted as a regular you were permitted to make a choice of one from three regiments. My first preference was the 4th Queens Own Hussars and that is what I got. I will refrain from revealing my 2nd and 3rd choice, for I would like to conduct myself as a gentleman and have no desire to upset (or disappoint) those fine regiments.

So, at last I was to travel to Colchester to join my regiment and upon arrival at HQ, I was registered and told to report to C Squadron who were in Cavalry Barracks. I met my troop sergeant and was allocated my bed but told not to unpack until I had an interview with the Squadron Leader (SL) the following morning.

The interview with the SL went very well and I met the Squadron Sergeant Major, who turned out to be a Geordie from Byker. He told me that after my first week being taught the Regimental History and what was expected of a 4th Hussar, he would be putting me on the Provost Staff, in other words he made me a Regimental Policeman (RP). My first reaction was "Oh hell!" But shortly after I heard that the RP's were free from training on the troopship, so I thought "that's me for a gentle voyage", or was I deluding myself? Read on and see.

Once registered and sorted I was granted a 7 day leave pass and so I set off to visit back home. What I did not realise at this point, was that this journey would mark the beginning of something else new in my life. I boarded the train into London Liverpool Street and transferred across to Kings Cross, where I'd catch the train back north to Newcastle. It was at Kings Cross where this amazing occurrence began. I was in uniform (as was the way in those days) and I was approached by a very attractive young lady dressed in an ATS (Auxiliary Territorial Service) uniform. She enquired whether I knew if this was the platform for the Newcastle train. "Yes" I replied. I asked if that was her destination, to which she gave an affirmative reply and so I asked if she was travelling alone, which she was. I figured that I couldn't miss out on an opportunity like this and so suggested that as we were both heading to the same destination, we could perhaps travel together. With a smile that was a mile wide she said, "why not?"

I had just met Betty, the lady that would one day become my wife. When reflecting in later years, on this our first encounter, we agreed that it was during this that we fell in love.

LAST MAN STANDING

We spent almost all the time together whilst back home, but as I had 7 days leave and she had 10, it was I who had to head back to the army first. Soon afterwards back at barracks, we were advised that we were being sent to Malaya. I was given 14 days Embarkation Leave. Betty was able to join me for the second half of this and she was there to see me off from Newcastle Central Station as I departed. We wouldn't see each other again for almost 4 years.

Leaving Southampton on Dilwara, The 4th Q.O. Hussars

The chopper to BMH, my mode of transport courtesy of Casevac

My armoured car at Beling

Me and my crew

Foot patrol

CHAPTER 3

The Fourth Queen's Hussars

I was back at barracks and on the evening of the 19th August 1948, the regiment departed by troop train from Colchester station to move to Southampton for transfer to the troop ship Dilwara. Our destination, Malaya.

As we had a man in detention who required an escort at all times, which was the duty of the regimental police, that's when I began to earn my pay. I still recall the ships departure, but at the time was rather pre-occupied with my duties. However, I was aware of a large crowd of well-wishers and the band of the 3rd Hussars cheering and singing us off to the popular song at that time Now Is The Hour. I could also see several our chaps who lived in the local area were quite affected by the occasion. Families and sweethearts thinking, will we ever see them again or will they return in one piece? Well regrettably a considerable number didn't, and that was what our political masters so blandly called an emergency (not a war).

Very soon we would enter the infamous Bay of Biscay, which should focus our minds to adjust to the considerable change in the motion of the ship. This would be rather uncomfortable for some.

LAST MAN STANDING

We had now begun a voyage that would last 36 days, and I would see the members of the regiment carrying out various exercises, such as physical, first aid, how to communicate without sound in the jungle and extra personal hygiene. As I was invariably on deck patrol or exercising our only prisoner, I was unable to take part, but I would watch and train in my own quarters to keep up with the rest. As the days came and went it began to become a bore as we had to work to a shift routine to ensure safety and security were maintained 24/7. We had the run of the ship. There were two decks, which were the accommodation for officers and some married families and therefore during the night any movement required silence and a lot of diplomacy. I will not elaborate further.

I will instead digress slightly to something on a much lighter note and in praise of British ingenuity. During the second world war, when people from what is now part of the EU were dropping bombs and trying to kill us, sometimes the bombs started fires and during those air raids it was necessary to have on hand an ample supply of water to deal with extinguishing the fires. The container comprised of a large steel frame with a large waterproof canvas trough that would be filled with water. They were very large and about 4-feet-deep. So, now the real story. I came on duty as deck patrol at 10.45hrs. I thought 'I will go forward on the starboard side and down aft on the port side'. I was unaware of the new contraption being on board, but I could hear the noise coming from the other side of the ship and thought it may be a tug of war contest. I then saw what I would know as an EWS (Emergency Water Supply). The noise was of a tightly packed mass of bodies in this trough with only their heads visible and water spilling over the top. It was just at that point an announcement came from the tannoy for dinner, and as if by magic there was no-one about. I slowly walked a very wet deck and had a look in the trough, only to discover there was about 3 inches of water left. Oh dear!

And so, we eventually arrived in Singapore, so bright, so colourful and oh my lord so hot. As I still had my prisoner, for he would not go to the CO until we were in our own camp, we were the first onto the ship at Southampton and the last off in Singapore.

The complete regiment were then transported to a huge transit camp at a place named Nee Soon, familiar to all army personnel who served in the area. The following morning our prisoner went before the CO and was remanded in that camp to await courts martial. Some readers may be curious to know, what became of the prisoner? In all honesty I have no idea, for he never returned to the regiment.

After that I was to report to the new Captain who had joined us shortly before we left the UK. He had spoken to me on several occasions when I was deck duty on the voyage, and it was during those brief conversations I got to like him and discovered that he had served in the Indian Army. He had acquired some jungle experience, which he hoped to put into practice at the first opportunity. He had sent for me to see if I would like to volunteer to join his troop. That was an easy decision. On joining the new troop, I knew most of them and I was pleased to see my friend Bill was one of the two Corporals and the Sergeant was an ex-World War 2 Army Commando with a hell of a pedigree.

Then the doors of hell opened, and training commenced with a bang. In fact, several of them. We had arrived at the Jungle Warfare School, staffed in the main by PTIs (Physical Training Instructors), Gurkhas, Eban Trackers and some very busy Medical Personnel. The training was quite ruthless and combined with the humidity and all the equipment, totally draining. On one occasion someone asked one of the PTI's "do you chaps never smile?" The response being "only on two events, when you pass out and if you drop down dead". The sad thing is, he would mean it.

And so, it went on and on. But as we approached the end of the course, we all began to feel fitter and wiser, and for enduring the training, everyone got a pass.

It was time to depart to Johor Baharu to rejoin the Squadron up north in the state of Negri Sembilan, at a town named Seremban. Two more days of lectures, then preparation to condition readiness for the call. And in 1948 that was not very long in coming. At about 02.00hrs we were roused from our slumber and ordered to get tooled up, we move in 15 minutes. We were on the move in 10, to the beginning of what could arguably be the worst day in my life. I was driving the scout car at the front of the troop (for those who are

17

not familiar, this is a small armoured two-man reconnaissance vehicle). With me was my friend Bill Thorburn, the troop Corporal. We were heading for a kampung (village) by the name of Kuala Kelawang. As we approached the area there were two sharp bends with steep banks. We considered them to be potential ambush positions and on the information we had received, suggested a section check the position on foot. This was carried out with our troops newly acquired speed and efficiency and Bill and I moved forward. From those bends to the kampung along a straight stretch of road, we could see people from the kampung running about and a small bus that was on fire. As we got closer we saw bodies, some smouldering. As Bill and I were dismounting, the rest of the troop arrived at this sight of horror and unimaginable cruelty. The CT's had torched the school bus with the children still onboard. My god, what sort of people are we fighting? Our officer, Cpt K, told us to usher the locals back to their homes and we would deal with the clear-up operation. That will remain with me to my dying day.

I do not wish to and will not elaborate further on the above incident. I would be remiss in not considering the readers possible feelings on such matters. For a member of the armed forces, there is always the risk that you will be confronted by dreadful sights or sounds, as sad to say it goes with the job.

We remained in the area until a platoon of the Malaya Regiment took over and we returned to HQ Seremban. No-one in our troop had any desire to discuss what had taken place at Kuala Kelawang and no-one at camp bothered us in the NAAFI. The following day I was stopped by the Sergeant Major. Being a Geordie, he asked if I was alright and I told him we were pleased that the other lads did not bother us in the NAFFI. "I gave them all a warning you were all to be left alone". I have often thought in tense situations humour in some form will emerge. It just so happens in our troop we had a lad from Sunderland and when the WO enquired "what was the Mackem like when the heat was on?" I said, "sorry sir, he was OK". Old habits die hard.

It was back to normal routine, i.e. foot patrols, road patrols, escort duties and stop and search operations. And occasionally, acting on information setting up an ambush. Sometimes successfully, but quite often boring and a complete waste of time. However, it was time to move on and the squadron had orders to go further north to relocate to Raub in the state of Pahang. This was the largest state in Peninsula Malaya. It is reported it was also the largest area of jungle, the majority of which being unmapped. Therefore, its remarkable size and density favoured the enemy more than us and for some time concealed several enemy training camps. I will return to this item later. For the moment, I shall digress to complete my own view of the geography of this very interesting, but in that period, extremely dangerous place. From west to east you travel through jungle, across rivers, past tin mines to Kuantan and beyond, to the beaches of the South China Sea, which today are my idea of Paradise. But sadly, at that time extremely advisable to avoid.

As the squadron settled in the town it was by then approaching Christmas. Our Sergeant Major arranged for the Jocks and Geordies to carry out the duties such as guard and any operational requirements on Christmas Eve and Day. Then it would be the others turn to do the same for us on New Year's Eve and Day. As we discussed our very limited enjoyment of the occasion, we were ordered on parade to hear some quite devastating news from Regimental HQ. 4th Troop of A Squadron had been ambushed near Sungai Seput with the loss of an Officer, a Corporal and six Troopers. That for me was a very significant blow, for among those troopers was my great friend Tom who enlisted with me back in 1947 and was now listed KIA (Killed in Action) New Year's Eve 1948/1949. God Bless you Tom. Needless to say, New Year was put on hold that year.

Each time I have returned to visit what I have come to think of as my second home, I have travelled to visit those graves who lie side by side in God's Little Acre, Batu Gajah. (We Will Always Remember Them).

Time did not stop that night, nor did the war on terrorism. Civilians and Police were being killed out there and our job was to put an end to it. We were ready to commence operations but this time with renewed determination plus a score to settle. Once more we didn't have long to wait.

Cpt K assembled the troop to inform us that we were going on detachment to Kuantan and would for a time be operating as an independent unit, but once more work in support of the local police in a large area to the east and north of the Pahang River, between Jerantut and Kuantan. Our first reaction "oh great, we will be beside the sea for some relaxation". Fat chance! It turned out there would be little opportunity for such delights. Come to think of it, a full night's sleep was a luxury. On arrival, Bill and I were ahead of the troop in our scout car on orders to locate our accommodation, which Bill had a map reference for. To our amazement it was an old abandoned Chinese Hotel, i.e. doss-house. When we returned to lead the troop, they all wanted to know what the accommodation was like. We told them it was a hotel and they were ever so pleased. But on arrival, much to Bill and I's amazement, they all turned quite nasty and began to throw things at us. Bill and I just could notunderstand and decided there's just no pleasing some people.

It did not take long to settle in and shortly after we received a visit from the OCPD (Officer Commanding Police District), who we would be working very closely with during our time in his vast command. A very nice gentleman.

He informed us that he had a small Police Post in a tin mining town west of Kuantan named Gambang, which was manned by four Malay PC's commanded by a very daring British Police Lieutenant. There was also another tin mine and British settlement at Sungai Lembing and that was the first task. We were asked to investigate and assess the best way to make access in and out. There was a stretch of the road where the density of the jungle was so thick, right up to the west side of the road and continued for approximately a mile and a half. This area had acquired the name of the "dirty mile and a half". Therefore, it was thought essential to clear that jungle back 100yds. The OCPD said he would arrange with PWD (Public Works Department) to carry out the work, with all haste if we provided the protection. In just over two weeks, the job was complete to everyone's satisfaction, the exception being the local CT unit, who must of started to look for some other soft target. So one could say a lot of the time, what we thought of as routine (another typically British understatement which encompassed both foot and road patrols, escorts and showing the flag), was a quite daunting task split between seventeen troopers and three NCO's, average age 19 years. But poor old Mick was much older and had taken part in the 2nd World War. He never complained, an example to all we young ones. Wherever you are Serg, God bless you for making us the team we became (Ment et Manu).

Bill and I's Alternative Mum and Dad
As it happened, it was at Sungai Lembing that one of the more pleasant interludes took place. Our leader, Cpt K, thought it may be an act of reassurance if we were to offer to stay for one or two nights in the British compound where the mine engineers and their wives lived. It covered quite a large area with their bungalows, tennis court and club. Cpt K's idea was for us to bed down in the club house, but our new friends had other ideas. They wanted to accommodate this troop two, to a house as their guests. This was unanimously agreed and that was the beginning of an unexpected, and may I say, truly heart-

warming period of our time in Malaya. Just imagine, we were between the ages of 18 and 20, thousands of miles from home. Bill and I felt we had acquired a family. Mrs & Mrs Black were our new mother and father, so kind and understanding. They had a small guest room which they prepared for us, a well-furnished bathroom plus a shaded veranda on which we could sit and chat after a wonderful home cooked dinner. We would talk of home and family and girlfriends. Mr Black and, as we would call his wife, Mum, both hailed from Scotland and had been prisoners of the Japanese after the fall of Singapore. They nevertheless had decided to see their lives out back at Sungai Lembing. Who could blame them? Sitting there on that veranda with your glass of Tiger beer, gazing at the surrounding jungle clad hills as the sun was going down. I recall on one occasion saying what an impressive sight it was and mum saying "yes, that's why we couldn't leave". Another time Bill and I were on our own, I was looking at the view and he was saying "the bastards are out there, we can't let these people down". Sad to say as is the life of the soldier, it was time to move on. But they were never very far from my mind, as you will learn later in this story.

Amongst our list of responsibilities when on our so-called normal routine and worth a mention here, we were often called upon to provide the escort to the Sultan of Pahang or his family.

I will now move on however to the day, sad to say I don't recall the date, that Cpt

K and the OCPD called the full troop together for a briefing. They were accompanied by a small Chinese young man. We were advised that he had surrendered to the police and was prepared to lead us to a large CT training camp, which was in deep jungle at the top of an area known as the Jabbor Valley. This chap who had brought the information to us was a cook. He assured the police that there was up to a hundred plus in the camp, with only one entry track, a sentry armed with a sub machine gun and two exit tracks on the west side unguarded. Therefore, the plan was that the police jungle squad would cover the exit track and our squad would deal with the sentry on the entry. We would move in at night without any noise. Our Eban tracker in the lead, the assault would commence at first light. The sentry had been taken out without a problem. Only two CT's managed to escape. Sadly, one of the police squad was killed and that put a damper on the operation. All the captured CT were handed over to the police, then we were free to return to our hotel.

Next and rather suddenly, everything seemed to go into overdrive. We received orders to pack up and move to Kuala Lumper (KL), re-join the rest of the squadron and prepare to move to Singapore to transfer to Hong Kong. Very nice I thought, but life never runs so smoothly and whilst preparing our vehicles for shipment, we were called away to a tin mining area north of KL by the name of Rawang. The urgency was that an ongoing operation was underway involving the Scots Guards driving through a large group of CT's from the area south of the Fraser Hill Gap, who were thought to be heading in the direction of Rawang. Our orders were to lay an ambush to cover the most likely escape route. So, we got tooled up and headed north to the tin mine. On arrival we dismounted, moved over the tin mine flats into the jungle and quickly located an ideal spot to set up the ambush. Oh, goody goody! This of all things, is just about the most unpleasant, uncomfortable, mind destroying and boring part of this type of jungle warfare. The only means of communication was by hand signal or, if close to the recipient, whisper, usually lying in a thousand years of decaying vegetation for days on end. Plus, insects capable of dealing you an unpleasant bite, the possibility of a passing snake and so many other rather unpleasant creatures. If you slept it would only be in brief spells. Oh, and let me not forget the leeches. After 24 hours, we were almost out of food and the officer in charge asked for two volunteers to go to the tin mine where there was food to collect and return. I and Paddy C jumped in, slipped off and made our way to the dredger. We had both emptied our small packs to enable us to collect the most food we could carry and a fair amount of water. We then set out to go back to the ambush position. I will at this point draw your attention to the fact that Paddy was armed with a Sten gun and I with a Mk5 303 rifle. I am drawing your attention to this as it now becomes relevant. The formation of the enemy would usually be to have a three-man scout party out front. We set out on our return walking across the flats toward the jungle. As we approached the end of the flats, there was a very steep incline. As we were negotiating this, right before us, the three-man enemy scouting party appeared. I don't know who was the most surprised, them or us. I shouted fire and commenced firing. Paddy was also firing but his Sten gun jammed. I must have got off ten rounds in record time and much to our amazement our visitors had gone. So, what to do now. Are they lying in wait for us? Paddy thought yes and at first so did I. But, after a period of about ten minutes had elapsed I began to think if they were the scouts, they would have to make the main body of their unit aware of our presence. So, the chances of them being a problem were somewhat reduced. We made a run for home which took us about 10 minutes. When we had got our breath back, the young officer in command of this ambush detail asked me for a report on the shooting incident. I gave it without hesitation, he accepted it with a thank you. You may recall when this action was called, we (i.e. the assault troop) were preparing to move and a few of us were instructed to take part in this operation. Being eager to re-join my own troop, I took advantage of the situation to hint that our roll was now probably surplus to requirement. The CT's were now aware of our presence in this area and would most likely avoid it like the plague. It was shortly after, that we were told to stand down and return to KL.

By the time we re-joined the squadron they were ready to move off for the, as it turned out, all too short a detachment to Hong Kong in support of 27 Brigade who were awaiting the arrival of an armoured unit from the UK. On arrival we moved into Ti Lam Camp, located on a cliff top overlooking the sea. But we were only there a very short time and then moved north to Lo-woo, close to the border between what had now become Red China and the New Territory. At this point the situation was relatively akin to a stand-off, all be it a little one sided. At the time I was thinking to myself, you have been in a similar situation before. It was that last job in Malaya prior to this move. You may recall that when Paddy and I came face to face with those three CT's, I fired my rifle and they ran away. Yet somehow deep down, I had this feeling it wouldn't work this time. We had been deployed at the only road crossing from Hong Kong and Canton situated in the centre of a small rather impoverished village. The actual crossing point was depicted by a large hinged wooden pole as a barrier. This no doubt begs the question how did they keep control of the comings and goings? Well about two miles south of this village you come to an enormous wire fence with huge steel gates and that is the place where checks were made.

It is well to point out that on that day, the Chinese Communist Army had just arrived at the border having overrun the Chinese Nationalist Army. But it would appear they had no territorial designs at the time. By the time all of this had settled down our replacement had arrived from the UK and we were ordered to return to Malaya to take up where we had left off.

Our return from Hong Kong was on the troop ship Empire Haladail. When we arrived in Singapore, we were soon moved back up country to link up with the Gurkhas at Kluang, for joint operations between the main north-south highway and the south china sea. In the main it was a bit boring but did often result in a dip in the sea at Mersing where there was a small RAF Regiment LEP (locally enlisted personnel) who always gave us a warm welcome. In particular their British Flight Sergeant who had all the characteristics of an early day Sergeant Bilko. He could sell fridges to Eskimos and had the local headman in his pocket. I am sure he went out of his way to impress us with items deemed impossible to obtain. On one occasion I jokingly challenged him to get me a bottle of Newcastle Brown Ale, which was unavailable out there at that time. On the next trip down there, which I was not on, on their return my mate Bill brought me two cans of Newcastle Brown. I found out much later cans were not available in the UK until sometime later. As I said - Bilko. Hey ho, all good things must come to an end.

It was shortly after this whilst on a follow up operation, a Chinese foreman on a local rubber estate was dragged off a local bus and taken into the jungle. When this was reported to the police, we were sent out on a follow up patrol. The bus driver took us to the point where they entered the jungle and we set off in pursuit. We had not gone far when we found where they had been waiting to carry out their abduction plan. As the light was beginning to fade hindering our pursuit, we decided to make use of the site and set out at first light to continue our endeavour to capture them or put them to the sword. Sad to say but when dawn arrived our plan was thwarted by the foe, for on moving off we found the badly mutilated body of the poor unfortunate Chinese foreman who had been abducted. We made radio contact with HQ to collect the body, then we moved on in an effort to catch up with the would-be tarnished perpetrators.

Our Eban tracker had no bother finding their track for it was so obvious, in fact a little too obvious for all of us. So, we made a stop to hatch a new plan and exchange our heavy equipment. This was to share the burden of carrying the rations and heavy weapons, and it was at that point things went downhill, for it was my turn to carry the rations. This was a task no-one liked to do as it involved having a lightweight metal frame strapped on your back onto which was attached a very heavy box of rations, most uncomfortable and disliked by all. But everyone would take their turn for that was our policy. Even Cpt K took his turn. At this juncture it was agreed that the track we were following was so obviously a trick to lead us into an ambush and would require a change of tactics. Cpt K always had a plan; this one involved a three-man reconnaissance section as opposed to the standard formation. So, we moved off until we reached a river where we were confronted with two more frustrations. The trail ended at the river and as we were coming to the end of the monsoon season the river was swollen, so did the quarries cross the river here or did they swim downstream?

It was decided that my best friend Bill would swim across to the other bank and ascertain if they had crossed there, or had they gone in the river and taken a chance? As

29

this was taking place, I was standing on the bank side when suddenly it gave way and sent me hurtling downhill towards the river. Bear in mind the weight that was on my back. I knew I was badly injured. This brought everything to a halt, and it was decided to call for a helicopter, and morphine. When the chopper arrived, it had to hover over the river as the jungle was too dense for the pilot to see the winchman and this would be the only way to get me out. That would be the last time I'd see Bill and the rest of my colleagues for the next 13 weeks. I was flown to BMH (British Military Hospital) Singapore and was immediately rushed into the operating theatre for, I was told, a considerable number of hours. Apparently in that fall I had sustained several internal injuries and loss of blood. Once more I had the good fortune to have the right people around to see me through. I must tell of my sojourn to Hotel BMH. It was as one would expect, all inclusive. Most of the staff were male, but there were also several very attractive and charming QAANC nursing sisters and after they had all had a go at throwing my body about, they informed me it was all part of the service. This was followed by a long period of strictly administered medication and a two-hour session of physiotherapy every day. It was while all this was taking place there was, unbeknown to me, a very special surprise being arranged. I would like to think that it may have been the best kept secret in the far east land forces.

Apparently one of the nursing sisters had noticed in my mail two letters and what could be a card and assumed it may be a birthday card.

Return from op

Inspecting enemy position we had overrun. K our
leader with Sten Gun

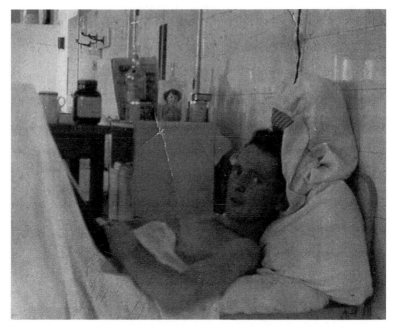

My sojourn in Hotel BMH, Singapore

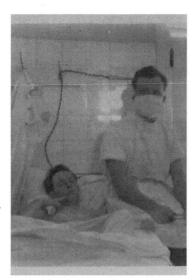

My sojourn in Hotel BMH, Singapore

This photo you will see at my bedside

LAST MAN STANDING

Now in this ward there were several members of my regiment, and they were asked if they could find out but not let me know. Well, one of the lads asked me and I told him it would be my 21st, "but keep it to yourself, don't tell the rest of the lads". I thought that would be the end of the subject. The card that had been the giveaway was from my girlfriend back home in England. This was now to be a very special time for me, on my actual birthday. It began much as any other day and at lunch time two of the medical orderlies put me in a wheelchair and took me to the day room. There were all the other patients, all the nursing staff and QAANC sisters. The room was decorated and there were lots of sandwiches and much more. They all sang happy birthday and following me into the room was the hospital cook with a birthday cake with 21 candles. The matron presented me with the key to the ward's beer cupboard for a short while, then the highlight of the party, a hug and a kiss off all the Queen Alexandra Sisters. It was truly a happy day.

Time was moving on and my condition was improving to the point where I would be discharged from this haven of care and comfort, or as the army would say RTU (Return to Unit).

It was time to say farewell to nursing staff and new friends and report to the RTO, Singapore Railway Station. The duty clerk at the RTO checked my movement orders, which had apparently been changed just before I arrived. I had set off under the impression that my squadron had moved from Kluang to Seremban, but the new orders were for me to go to KL, as my troop was on a special assignment and they would collect me at the station on my arrival. At this stage my spirits were high at the prospect of meeting up with Bill and the rest of my brothers.

While in the RTO's office an officer came in and enquired as to whether I had arrived for the train and the clerk pointed me out. He came over and I could see that he was as young as me and had only just arrived. He was a 2nd Lieutenant RASC on his way to Taiping and as was the practice at that time, all military personnel were on duty and under the command of an officer appointed. My thoughts on this going north (fresh off the ship) to south (the voice of experience). To return to this officer, he left me totally amazed when he asked me to stick close at hand. The RTO had told him to ask for me. When I said that I was sorry but did not understand, the clerk had told him "he's one of K's boys, no sweat, you will be fine". I thought "what the hell has been going on in my absence, are we building a reputation for ourselves?" On arrival in KL after an uneventful journey, I was met by my friend Bill and to my surprise Cpt K our leader came to greet me (this was the measure of the man). He truly cared for his men, god bless him, an Officer and Gentleman.

Then back to camp and a Tiger (beer) reception with all my brothers. We were a family, have no doubt. The next day dawned and I was back on duty to learn what this special assignment was. Apparently, the British Government of the day were sending a delegation of ministers to assess the situation in Malaya

34

and we had the task of protecting them. In other words, more escort duty with unnecessary bull****, but we just obey and carry on. To be honest we all detested the task and felt there were more important things we could be attending to, rather than nursing a lot of MPs being hosted and pampered whilst there were innocent people out there being killed and we should be out there trying to stop that.

In all that situation lasted for a month, thank the Lord. We then returned to normal routine, until we got an order that we should join the squadron as they travelled north to RHQ in Ipoh. This was to take part in the periodical training programme, neither enjoyed nor welcomed by all. At last it was over, and we moved off to Taiping, where there was awaiting a totally unexpected shock, not only for me but the rest of the troop. It appears the Regimental Signal Sergeant was returning to the UK and as Bill was quite an expert in that field, he was to join HQ. So, we lost him to RHQ. There was much sadness within the troop. Cpt K had tried to keep him with the troop, but the CO was insistent that Bill had to go.

This decided, I was given the job of driving him to the railway station at Taiping and picking up his replacement, Trooper Angus Fraser, a Scot who was well known to all the troop. I say this with some reservation for Angus was a mickey taker, practical joker and the biggest leg puller in the world. He became the troop leader's operator and my friend.

Our camp at Taiping was an open one and

difficult to guard. There was a backdrop of very high hills and guard duties were very challenging, but there was only one incident of the CT's attempting to breach the perimeter which was quickly dispersed by a burst of gunfire from one of our armoured cars browning machine guns.

It may appear to the reader that I had very quickly forgotten my friend Bill. Not so, for this was the army and we were soldiers. He had left us at the request of the CO, and for the guidance of those who are not familiar with military protocol – a request from the CO is a camouflaged order – therefore it is our duty to obey. Have no fear, he will return but in much different circumstances. One must wait to see. No one could forget Bill.

Cpt K called all the troop to what was referred to as an O group. The object of these gatherings was to ensure everyone was fully aware of the part they had to play, and inform those who had specific tasks to perform, such as cooking, ensuring batteries for the wireless and if the operation requires a sentry to be taken out, that the person who would carry out that task had all the necessary expertise. A task usually given to the troop sergeant, but his time was up, and he was awaiting his replacement. So, the problem of a sentry removal was solved by the troops strong man, a very likeable Welshman who I shall refer to as MG. To continue, this gathering was not for an upcoming operation as we thought, but to once more go out on detachment to join up with the Gurkhas on a long-term full operational attachment.

The troop received this news with great enthusiasm for we could wish for nothing better. Therefore, after collecting our necessary stores and equipment, we left the squadron destination Sungai Petani, to meet our cheerful comrades the Gurkhas. We headed west then north arriving to a traditional Gurkha welcome who, in their typical way, assisted us to move our kit and bedding into our billet. You have got to believe me it was truly wonderful, such a memorable episode.

The following day dawned. It was usually breakfast at 07.00hrs, but as we normally exercise in our own camp, we would have our breakfast at 08.00hrs and exercise at 07.00hrs. This conformed with our new friends, but as it happens, we were ordered to forget exercise that morning as we were meeting the Sungai Petani Police Jungle Squad. We did this on Cpt Ks orders. He said it was a familiarising exercise, but we think it was to give him an opportunity to assess them. As it turned out they were very accomplished, so we returned to camp and had a most enjoyable afternoon entertaining the Gurkha children in the married quarters play area.

We commenced with a game of football against the boys with the girls as spectators. It wasn't long before the girls got so excited that they joined in. We had arranged before the kick-off we would let the boys win, but it would appear the young ladies had other ideas and supported us, which I am sure gave the boys an advantage. We lost thanks to the intervention of those sweet little darlings, but it was all good fun. The children absolutely loved it and wanted more. These interludes gave us some respite from living on the edge. Unfortunately, such intervals were few and far between, making them all the more enjoyable. For those who are curious we did play a return match without the help of our little darlings – and still lost.

So, it was back to work after our brief sojourn in our new home. This commenced with an extended road patrol along the I77 to Alor Setar and to the Siam border. When I said extended, I was referring to the length of time we spent assessing some areas of interest to see if they could be a problem at some later date. It is worth noting that Cpt K was a stickler for detail and observation, particularly concerning people in the kampungs or on the side of the road. If you walk around them or just look very closely to see if they get edgy or nervous and if so, then you take them to one side and establish their identification. This could be relatively simple for by this time the whole nation had been registered and were always required to carry their ID card. Failure to do so would result in apprehension and placed in custody for further investigation, normally carried out by Special Branch Officers.

It is worth me clarifying here, the reason and necessity for this practice. In 1949 a law was introduced that all citizens were required to register and at all times carry their ID card. It had been a mammoth task but was now bearing fruit, as it permitted the security forces to make those situations clearer. The campaign was unlike any other up to or at that time. For a start, the population had become multinational with labour being brought in from China and India. Unfortunately, this presented us with a challenge in how we could interact with these people and I will have to take any criticism for what I am about to write.

We had to be conscious that the civilian wing of the terrorist force that we were dealing with from the onset of the campaign (the Min Yuen), operated very much as an "underground" unit. It included people who had infiltrated themselves into the immigrant population. This made it very difficult to know or judge who was friend or foe. It could be a chap who comes around the camp selling ice cream, or the men who removed the refuse, or the very cheerful fellow in your favourite local cafe. They were all suspects in this game of life or death. But we quickly adapted to this situation. On reflection it is possible any or all these people were alright. That is and has been a problem and indeed I had several very dear friends who are of Chinese origin. several of those very brave Special Branch Officers were Chinese. It became abundantly clear to me that there was divided loyalty within the Chinese community. As to the effectiveness of our input, I was and still am not totally convinced. I am sure there are some still about who served out there at that time, who would disagree with my thinking. However, I have always based my view on what results we had in comparison with those fearless Special Branch Officers of Malaya Police.

I had the honour and privilege to meet some of them years later when I was their guest on National Police Day, an invitation and honour I shall forever cherish.

Hopefully those at home and elsewhere who were not aware of this extremely dangerous supply chain and perpetrators of death and fear, would not realise the increased pressure that was placed upon those who were involved in this conflict. But it pleases me to be able to say that no one cracked under the pressure. There is an old saying – "*self-praise is worthless*". But I have to report nevertheless that this saying did not get in the way on the many times when we had successfully completed an operation. There would be the mandatory Tiger party. And for those who were prepared to listen, many grisly exaggerated tales of daring do, some of them accepted, but the rest bull****. They were always delivered dramatically as is expected of an old soldier, well older than the one who is listening.

We were by now entering our fourth year and beginning to think of home and the girls we left behind, but just carried on with patrols on foot or by road. The only incident I would consider worthy of inclusion occurred whilst escorting a convoy travelling from Kuala Kangsar to Gerik via Lenggong. There was nothing unusual about that, it was a routine occurrence. The object of our involvement was, apart from the rations, there were weapons, ammunition and explosives plus medical supplies, all destined for the two commando units one at Lenggong and one at Gerik. This meant going deep into the

LAST MAN STANDING

Bad Lands; this is the real shooting gallery. Gerik is the farthest and quite close to the Thai border. We had never been involved in this task in the past, it was a different setting to our normal role. Then when Cpt K held his O group, he explained that we were brought in as the indications were that there was to be an attempt to launch a heavy attack on the convoy. He then went on to tell us before we set off, that he knew he could rely on all of us to conduct ourselves in the true tradition of the Regiment. "This will be our biggest engagement to date and all the pent-up frustration that I know you have locked up inside will be released, think of Kuala Kelawang. That said, the blood was up and we were raring to go.

We left Sungai Petani at 04.40hrs accompanied by a platoon of Gurkhas, a most reassuring sight to see. Driving through to Taiping in the early morning we arrived at the Malaya Regiment camp at 08.00hrs. We then had a compo breakfast along with our Gurkha friends who listened to what had taken place at Kuala Kelawang. Some of them drew their kukris and called out the battle cry "Ayo Gukhale!" The convoy arrived from Ipoh at 10.00hrs, with its escort from our own regiment's HQ. In the lead a scout car from reconnaissance troop and sitting proudly up front none other than a beaming Corporal Bill Thorburn. He was immediately swamped by his former comrades, or should I say long-lost brothers. For that is exactly what he was to everyone in the troop. But it was time to move off, the time was 11.00 hrs. The first stage was to Lenggong and we arrived at 12.00hrs. We were with a troop of 42 commandos.

41

The marines unloaded their consignment, which was mostly rations and some medical supplies, leaving us to have a brew. Then it was time to move on, the time 12.45hrs. A quick word from Cpt K, all weapons loaded and cocked, safety catches off after we had cleared the town. The first two or three miles were what I would term as comfortable, in so much as the road followed the course of the river with fairly flat terrain, cultivated with rice and a small amount of rubber. Not the ideal setting for an ambush. So, one becomes just a little relaxed until we crossed a trestle bridge that spanned the river. Beyond the crossing the river veered to the left away from the direction of the road and as the river became lost from view, we were now in dense jungle.

Everyone was silent and watching. I myself was thinking it could be any second now that tranquillity could be shattered by a hail of bullets heading in our direction. As we had now travelled some distance toward our destination, I and others were beginning to feel that they hadn't taken the bait, when about 5 miles from Gerik all hell broke loose. Very heavy small arms fire was raining down on us. I saw Cpt K running over the road to take shelter under the bankside and shouting orders to use the cover of the bankside. Jim, our radio operator, was with me and we made a run for cover just as Cpt K and Angus threw two grenades. Both exploded, probably injuring or driving the CT's off and giving us time to relocate our position to the top of the embankment, where we were joined by three Gurkhas who had a Bren gun. By this time Cpt K and Angus had reached our position.

LAST MAN STANDING

Also, at that time our sergeant and the men in
his APC had driven the enemy off the other end
of the bank top. It was all over in about 15
minutes. Casualties: two of our chaps had to
be hospitalised, the Gurkhas none. Enemy, two
dead and they must have had several wounded
judging by the number of bloody trails there
were leading away from the site of the attack.
We were later informed that a follow up party
had discovered four more bodies who obviously
had been members of the attackers' group. They
will not threaten anyone again that's for
sure. So, for us it was return to barracks the
following morning. As for our own casualties
they were transferred to BMH Kamunting, their
injuries being bad but not life threatening.
As the hospital was in Taiping and we were in
Sungai Petani, we all thought there would be
little chance of visiting our friends. When we
mentioned this to Cpt K he replied that he had
been working on that very subject and thought
he may have a solution. He had put forward an
idea to reconnoitre the area north of Gerik
to the Thai border. We had to establish the
possibility we could not negotiate the road
with British army vehicles because of the
narrow bailee bridge. Low and behold Cpt K had
the answer. They were most probably installed
during the Japanese occupation during WW11.
There were many such bridges in Burma. So that
would account for the presence of the would be
bailee bridge, but it appeared there were no
more bridges of that type further north. The
approximate distance to the border from the
bridge was roughly 7 miles. We only had a short
length of time to walk there and return to our
vehicles on the south side of the damned bridge,

with a corporal and 5 troopers for protection. So off we set at 04.30hrs doing a speed march hoping to gain some time. We used the road such as it was, but on the way back, as there was no shade, it became very uncomfortable. Whatever we were taught at Johor Bahru, came in very useful. I can say that on arrival everyone was totally drained, needless to say, except for Cpt K.

We returned to Gerik and our Royal Marine hosts for a well-deserved rest and a wholesome meal. Then after a most enjoyable evening and a good night's sleep, we assembled on the vehicle park to receive our orders for our return to Sungai Petani. Cpt K informed us we had been asked to give two government surveyors a lift as far as Taiping. This was working out very well, for it allowed us time to visit our friends at the BMH Kamunting. They were delighted to see us and as you could well imagine bombarded us with many questions and thanked us for the consignment of Tiger that everyone contributed to. Their news was that one of them would be re-joining the troop very soon. After much hand shaking and patting on the back it was time to depart to home base. This was an uneventful journey, although to round it off the Gurkha families came out to greet us, everybody wanting to help us get back into our billet. So nice, but they really didn't need to. Once completed, it was time for weapons cleaning, washing down and a general check over of the troop's vehicles, then time for dinner.

No sooner had we settled down back at

LAST MAN STANDING

Sungai Petani, we were ordered to move to the Cameron Highlands. The purpose being the daily escort from Tana Rata to Tapah Road Station. This was just to let the enemy know they will not be permitted to disrupt the access to this thriving area of this beautiful part of Malaya. So once more we had to say our farewells. This was probably the most moving and emotional departure we ever had to make for there were the dear Gurkha children all in line and as we drove by them the boys stood saluting and the girls waving and crying and all we could do was wave back and try to smile. They must have all taken a shine to us, for I did notice some wives were shedding a few tears. We all hoped we would see them once again and off we went to the Cameron Highlands. We stopped for a brew at Tapah, before ascending to Tanah Rata to our new home, an old abandoned bungalow located on the edge of the golf course. We had been briefed by Cpt K before leaving Sungai Petani. This is how we would have to work: the troop would be divided into two groups and there will be no convoy on a Sunday. The half who were not on convoy duty would be on standby. If the convoy was subjected to an ambush, the drivers and radio operators would report to 45 Commando on the opposite side of the golf course, pick up two fighting crews and go to the assistance of the convoy under attack. But as the CT's had been hounded in the last few months, it appears they had gone to ground.

At this point I am made aware that it has become necessary for me to go to hospital, as I have been diagnosed with amoebic dysentery and so I was admitted to BMH Ipoh. I was confined there for a month, then transferred to the British Army Convalescent home at Tanah Rata. I began to get very worried. Why? The Regiment were packing to go home and here am I stuck in this convalescent home. As my troop were still on detachment some of them would call and have a chat when they could. I took the opportunity to pass on my concern that I may be overlooked and left behind. This prompted a visit from Cpt K. This was not unusual, for he always had a policy of never leaving his men uninformed. He told me that he had arranged with the matron to hold up my discharge to coincide with the convoy that would arrive to meet up with our night train to Singapore. At that point I would be met by the duty driver, to transport me to the transit camp at Nee Soon. The object of all this; that it was to be a member of 5 Troop, C Squadron, 4th Hussars, who would be the last man to leave Malaya. Well, Cpt K's plan went almost as planned, but he had not accounted for the fact that our regiment had now been replaced by the 12th Royal Lancers. On my arrival at convoy assembly point, I was confronted by a very young and nervous subaltern from the Lancers, who greeted me with a look of relief on his face, and said "thank god, an experienced soldier". He wanted to know if I had taken part in the convoy escort duty or, was I being transferred to the 12th Lancers. My blood began to boil and with as much restrain as I could muster I replied "No sir, I already have the honour to serve in the finest cavalry regiment in the British Army and perhaps the world, and to the best of my knowledge the only all regular regiment in that army when we left the UK four years ago. So, if you wish I will

travel in the last APC". And off we went to Tapa
Road Station. The trip was uneventful, so when
we arrived at the Malaysia Regiments camp all I
could do was stay there until the night train
arrived at 18.00hrs. There I met up with the
train commander who was an officer from the
Manchester Regiment. His first remarks were "I
thought your lot were away home". When I told
him how I came to be here he burst out laughing
and said, "I bet you were sweating" and told me
to pick my spot. When I said, "the back veranda"
he looked rather puzzled and asked was there
any particular reason why there, I realised he
had a sense of humour and replied, "to avoid
nosy people asking a lot of questions". Thank
goodness he took it in the right spirit, and
he did come and see me during the night. He
also sent one of his men along with a mug of
tea. Just as the sun was rising, he came to say
goodbye to me in the RTO's Office. A very nice
gentleman. Then appearing in the office doorway
Trooper Peit Surddy, the duty driver to take me
to camp at Nee Soon and once more I was with the
troop. One could sense the excitement all over
the camp. I had an interview with the squadron
leader and Cpt K. Both instructed me to take a
few days off to readjust and prepare my kit for
the voyage home. This was much appreciated, and
I went down into the kampung and got measured
for a dress uniform. To me that was preparing
for an impending wedding for I am heading back
to darling Betty who has waited all these years
for my return, never failing me.

CHAPTER 4

Going Home

We were told that we would be sailing in ten days' time and to everyone, those ten days seemed to last forever. But at last we were on the move and boarded ship, the Empire Windrush. We sailed at 16.00hrs. I still remember thinking as we entered the Strait of Malacca and the light was fading but the onshore lights were twinkling, there's not so many going home as came out. I wondered if I would ever return and it was just about then I was joined by Angus. He said, "I bet I know what you have been thinking" and he was correct, as our thoughts were the same. It was then some of our colleagues enquired if there had been something worth watching so we told them our thoughts. All agreed we should do something. It was decided that we would stand in line facing the shore and we all said words to the effect "Sleep Well Bonnie Lads".

So, we were on our way home and for me to the one I love. But it will take 36 days to Southampton. You may well imagine; it feels like a lifetime of sheer boredom and very little to do. There was a brief period of excitement as we travelled through the Mediterranean. There was an announcement over the ships tannoy that open decks would be out of bounds to all but members of the regiment, as we were about to pass through a very heavy storm rated force 10. Well as predicted it arrived on time and for some it made life just a little more uncomfortable for a short time. It left those poor unfortunates suffering from mal de mer to worry about the Bay of Biscay. I cannot help but feel sorry for those who are affected by this condition. After we rode out the storm, we had to make an emergency stop at Algiers to evacuate a chap who was suffering from peritonitis. I didn't know him he was a member of A Squadron and by all accounts he survived and re-joined the regiment later the following year.

The journey back whilst by and large boring, had little moments of what felt like highlights of a sort, such as the Rock of Gibraltar. There were deck games organised and routine inspections, boat drills and now and then a lecture or training film. There was no shore leave as there was potential trouble in the Canal Zone. To the best of my knowledge, I don't think that this created a problem for anyone, we just wanted to get home and because we were now into December, get home for Christmas.

I can't explain the feeling of joy at seeing the coastline of England as we arrived in the channel after almost four years. It was cold but we didn't give a damn, we would be home for Christmas and I'd be back with the girl I love. Two whole months disembarkation leave, then hopefully a decent spell in the UK.

That brings me to the end of my Far East Adventure. In truth perhaps a little boring and I'm sorry if it comes across that way. It is not my intention to over dramatise things of that nature, in that type of campaign. The dramatic incidents only happened at intervals. Much of our time was spent on strength draining jungle operations. In the beginning it was like chasing shadows, for the enemy had the advantage of years of experience in combating the Imperial Japanese Army. Ironically, they were using weapons supplied by the British, which were supposed to be handed back on the termination of hostilities. But we were soldiers and that was our task, so we did the job.

That was not uppermost in my mind at that moment, with Southampton in sight my spirits and anticipation were on the rise as we had to spend the night on board ship and be prepared to disembark at 05.30hrs in the morning. Needless to say, few of us went to sleep that night. Now a very brief description of the baggage a soldier had to carry on moving by troopship. There were two; one universal and one sea kit bag. Fortunately, on this occasion we did not have any weapons to carry so with one kit bag on each shoulder it was comparatively easy navigating the gangway. We then had to form up in three ranks in open order with the contents of both kit bags arranged in front for the customs officer to check. I had 18.00 cigarettes and I declared the lot. The officer asked if I was having a smoke out when I got home, smiled and moved on. Then when all this was completed it was time to get aboard the troop train that was alongside the customs shed, which will transport us to Tidworth and our new barracks. It was not a long journey and I think with being up early most of us fell asleep. On arrival at Tidworth everyone loaded their kit bags onto trucks and the regiment

Military Cemetery, Taiping

Me, pictured right,
with one of my
'brothers'

LINE-UP – Dave, middle row, third from the right, with his Troop of the 4th Hussars

We survived – but more to good luck than judgement

The 'band of brothers' Taiping

had to fall in to march to their new barracks. Being a garrison town, a lot of locals turned out to welcome our home coming.

We were impressed with the refurbished barracks. The bedsheets and the little bedside rug, ten beds to a room, two bathrooms and one shower. Oh, I almost forgot, each man had his own locker and a pillow with pillowcase. So, this is Monty's new modern army. A much-appreciated change from the days before our departure four years ago. More importantly it was time to collect our leave pass, travel warrant and bank book. Then off we all went for 52 days leave. First stop the Union Jack Club in London, where we booked in for the night. Dinner, then it was party time big style. We almost took the club over but caused no trouble. And so, to bed. Up at 06.30hrs, breakfast 07.30hrs, a proper English breakfast. I shared a table with Angus and Scrotey, another member of the squadron, who wanted to know what time we had to be back on the boat. Angus and I just looked at each other in speechless disbelief. Eventually Angus shook his head and said, "some things never change". I hope my smile was not too obvious for I was thinking "my god Angus has to deal with that all the way to Scotland". I can only hope there's no buffet car on their train.

So, it was goodbye to London, as I headed north to meet my future wife. I knew where she would be, so I planned to surprise her. The train journey was quite enjoyable, Angus and I discussed our plans for the next two months. Thank goodness, Scrotey slept the whole way. As we approached Newcastle, a sight that is sure to arouse the emotions of any true Geordie and upon crossing the High Level Bridge, there was that view of the River Tyne and the world-renowned Tyne Bridge. Every Geordie knows he is home. It was also time to bid goodbye to my Brothers in Arms. For four years they had been my family. As I was leaving the station there were several, what I took to be families, who were looking for sons or relatives returning with the regiment. They mentioned some names I recognised, one or two I did see in London who may be on a later train. As there was no-one to meet me, I got a taxi and went home. On arrival I was told that my father and sister had been at the station but had to leave as it was getting rather late for my young sister, but she was still up. We went through the greetings and the hugs, cups of tea and then everyone was sleepy, so it was off to bed.

CHAPTER 5

The Reunion

Well, the next day dawned and my excitement was boundless for this is the day I will be reunited with my darling Betty. So off I went to call at her home to be met by her mother. I received a warm welcome from that lovely lady. A big hug and "when are you going to propose to her?" I gave her an assurance "at the very earliest possible moment, but we must find a home of our own". I then added "are we not assuming that is what she would want?" She replied "are you joking? She has talked about nothing else for the last four years". She went on to say that she had a request and little old naïve me replied "anything, tell me". Well yes, she certainly did and went on to tell me she wanted grandchildren. To say I was extremely embarrassed was obvious, but she laughed and apologised for shocking me.

Well, the clock was ticking round to the time of Betty's arrival home. Her mum heard the key in the door and told me to go into the other room. I heard Betty ask, "Has there been word from Dave yet?" her mum said, "No but something has been delivered, I put it in the other room". Betty asked what it was, and her mum said, "it's for you, go and see for yourself". And there was me thinking come on, open the door. Well, she did and rushed into my arms and soon began to weep. I said, "I don't look that bad, do I?". She replied, "No, it is just the number of times it was announced on the news that someone had been killed or injured and I would pray it was not you". I told her I must have been protected by her prayers and the fact I was very good at taking cover.

Jane, Betty's mum, was so thoughtful and said she had to pop out for something nice for tea. We both knew this was a ploy to leave us alone for a while. I suppose we were a little shy. I am sure we were both overcome with emotion and just stood hugging each other, savouring this very special moment that could never be repeated. Her mum returned and after tea I suggested that Betty and I go into Newcastle, as it had been so long since I had the joy of walking the streets. Betty agreed. I had a tidy up, she got changed and off we went. Unfortunately, this was mid-December and it was cold and dark, so I suggested we go to the NAAFI Club. This was great as there was a dance on, and as we both enjoyed dancing. We danced the night away.

The dancing and NAAFI tavern closed at 10pm, so we walked back to Betty's home by which time it was about 11.40pm. We sat and cuddled-up on the stairs before I had to leave to walk home to my mothers, about three miles away. So, I was ready for that and the sleep I would have when I got home. In all honesty I was walking on air and our love never faltered.

And so, life became a joy and pleasure. I would be waiting to meet her coming home from work, then we would have dinner together. Now and then we'd go to the NAAFI Club for a meal and some nights we'd stay for the dance. On my first Saturday home, Betty and I went to Newcastle for her to choose her engagement ring. From there we went to the Tatler Restaurant on Northumberland Street and that evening we went dancing at the Embassy Ballroom at Forest Hall. Very soon the memory of the last four years was forgotten and for a while so was the army. I could think of nothing but Betty and what the future held for us. We began to make plans for our future by opening a joint account and planned for a June wedding. This would give us time to find somewhere to live, as we did not want to live in with relatives. We sought some advice from our local MP, which turned out to be a total waste of time.

It was open knowledge by now that Betty's mum was terminally ill with cancer. My suggestion that we apply for a married quarter and Betty get a job in the NAAFI shop, had to be knocked on the head. For the time being I could do nothing until the end of my leave and see if the regiment can give me some sort of assistance.

In the meantime, I spent most of the time attending to Betty's mum to allow her to go to work. It was not a chore, for she was a sweet and very humorous lady. She never made a complaint; it was heart-breaking to see someone whose life is ebbing away before my eyes and be unable to offer any practical help. Our lives appear to have ground to a halt. We longed for the evenings when Betty would be home, and I would have prepared a meal for the two of us and something for Jane. Her food had to be puréed or liquidised. Easier said than done, but good fortune came my way in the form of a District Nurse who provided me with the necessary guidance for preparing this sort of meal. She even loaned me a liquidiser. A very nice lady and credit to her profession.

It would soon be time to return to army life which would mean Betty having to leave work until I can sort something out back at barracks. Without further ado I was off to Tidworth leaving a tearful Betty and Jane, I had to try to pull all the right strings to seek a solution to the current situation.

After a very boring and frustrating journey, I arrived at Tidworth to discover I was the first one to return. I decided not to waste any time and made my way to the Squadron Office in the hope of getting an interview with the OC, only to be informed that he had gone to Warminster and wouldn't be back until that night. My spirits dropped, but as I left the office and was about to open the door, who should walk in but nonother than my Troop Leader Cpt K. His first words were "by god you must be keen, there's no action out there". I am sure I must have managed a smile; I think I replied with something like, "I'm sure your right, but it's in the office I need some action". Cpt K asked me if he could be of any assistance. I told him of the situation. He said he would try to help, he would do his best, but could give no guarantee. So, I wandered back to my room in full depression. Next morning the SSM told me to be at the Squadron Office for the SL wanted to see me at 10.30hrs. I reported to the Squadron Office at 10.25hrs and after five minutes the SSM marched me in. The Squadron Leader informed me "you have a compassionate problem that you hope we can resolve for you. As it happens it is possible that something can be arranged". He then went on to inform me that Cpt K had submitted a recommendation for my promotion. "This appears to coincide with your predicament and an ERE (extra regimentally employed) posting for a PSI (Permanent Staff Instructor) at the TA Centre, Newcastle upon Tyne. The only problem is that this requires a Sergeant". You can imagine how my spirit went from high to low. He went on, "In accordance with Kings Regulations, I cannot promote you from trooper to sergeant in one. But I can make you a lance sergeant and if you do a good job, I can make you substantive after 6 months. That will put you on full sergeants pay. Would that make life a little easier for you?".

I just could not believe that this was happening. As if it was an afterthought, he said "I hope this will persuade you to take a twelve-month extension when your time is up next year". I assured him that I was sure that would not be a problem. Then I thought "I think I will, but only if that's what Betty wants".

Next day I moved into the Sergeants Mess, collected my new stripes from the QM's store and had them stitched onto my uniforms by the Regimental tailor. You may well imagine how my emotions were, I'm sure in freefall. Then there was the mickey taking from all my brothers in the troop.

Then I was officially welcomed to the sergeant's mess by the RSM. There was much hand shaking, patting on the back, and wanting to know what I would like to drink. But I have been around the block too many times to fall for that one.

The problem of getting news to Betty was somewhat fraught with complications. There were no postal facilities at my location and no convenient telephone service at Betty's location. However, eventually and after much heart-searching I managed to make phone contact with her local shopkeeper, who was more than happy to ask her to come to the phone. She was overjoyed and so excited and wanted to know when I would be home. As this was Wednesday, I hoped to be home by Sunday then I could report to the Adjutant at TA HQ Newcastle on Monday.

Therefore, it would seem I have opened a new chapter in my life, hoping I can adapt to this part-time soldiering. But that was for another day, this was the here and now and it is time to go out with my old friends, my Brothers, and off we all went to the Ram in Tidworth for a fantastic night of great reminiscing and remembering lost friends.

CHAPTER 6

Tyneside

Well, the day of my arrival at my new place of work dawned. I met the present RSM, a nice chap, who was almost at the end of his service. He was a WWII veteran and former POW. It was at this point I was to learn that he was to be replaced by a WO1 from my regiment who in my early days was my troop sergeant. An all-round good chap. It made me think "do they send them here before putting them out to pasture?" I wondered what the hell am I doing here but stopped short of taking any action and decided to settle into my job.

I was introduced to the adjutant who was a Captain. He appeared very friendly and we had a very long discussion on his and my role in the administration of a very proud TA Regiment which had a remarkable outstanding wartime record; South Africa, WWI and WWII. There were three squadrons HQ, A, B, C. They also had their own medical unit, plus the LAD. There was a PSI with each squadron and a regular RSM at HQ.

After one week I found the admin staff were of a very high standard. The remainder, at this point shall I say, leaving much to be desired. Needless to say, I did not have a feeling of excitement at the prospect of attempting to get them into shape. I just consoled myself that the new RSM would arrive any time soon. Once more this came as an added bonus, for he was my first troop sergeant on joining the 4th Hussars and he and his brother were on the regimental police with me at Colchester before we went to Malaya.

Tom, the new RSM, arrived on the Monday and had a long discussion with the CO and the Adjutant. After about 40 minutes I was called in to be briefed on assisting the RSM who had undertaken organisation of the forthcoming presentation of a new Guidon. This is a classic ceremony, which will attract a large number of the public. The ceremony would be held in Fenham Barracks, followed by a parade and march past in Newcastle's Eldon Square. Afterwards there would be a buffet lunch at the Barracks. For such a project it will require a great deal of training and rehearsal to achieve the very high standard required. It would be deemed wise to have a second Drill Instructor to assist the RSM. Therefore, I was very quickly dispatched to the 2nd Battalion Scots Guards to undertake a Drill Instructors course.

I could not claim to be overly thrilled at the prospect of square bashing after all these years but had to console myself that I could get through this course and get back to Betty and home. So, it was off to Elisabeth Barracks, Pirbright for a ten-day DI course. The course is designated for WO's and Sergeants and the class was conducted by a Sergeant from the Scots Guards, a very good instructor and in all respects a nice chap. I am bound to say that for I came away from the course with distinction and a small trophy.

LAST MAN STANDING

Sad to say on my return home I was informed that Jane, Betty's mum, was slipping away. There was very little time left. Talk about mixed emotions. I wished that dear lady to live but no-one could stop her pain. Little thinking I would have to contend with similar circumstances once more in later years. But I had to get on with my job. By now Betty had been granted sick leave so now we were managing, and I usually got home about 3.00pm. We were as happy as could possibly be under the existing conditions. If it was not for the fact poor Jane was so unwell, we would be so happy. At long last Betty's father turned-up. He and I had an in-depth discussion, after which he agreed to stay at home so that Betty could go back to work. Once this had been settled life became easier and allowed us to bank some money for our home. It was shortly after that poor Jane passed away. My feelings were of, thank God no more pain for her and no more suffering for the family. Our Loss Gods Gain.

But life goes on. When I reported the matter to the RSM, he told me to take three days off and he would inform the CO and if I needed any help, I was to ring him.

The first thing was to register the death and much to my amazement Betty's father said he would do the running about doing the arrangements and left Betty and I to organise a buffet for after the funeral, the flowers and let friends and relatives know.

In an attempt to lift Betty's spirits, I took her out for dinner to our favourite little

63

restaurant in Newcastle. We went here before I went to Malaya. We both loved it and our special waitress was on hand to serve and make our evening rather special.

But next day dawned and I accompanied Betty as she went to choose the flowers and called at the Addison Pub to book a room for after the funeral for old friends to meet. They could talk about times gone by and the great qualities Jane had in abundance, such as her never failing sense of humour, which would light up a room in an instant, along with many other features of her character. An unusual lady who would be widely missed by all who knew her. God Bless You My Dear Friend. I will not elaborate on the funeral other than to say it was attended by Betty, her father, myself and a group of friends, some of who came to the gathering at the Addison later. I have on occasions since thought that she didn't receive the respect that she deserved.

We now had to move on. Betty went back to work, and I resumed my duties at the TA centre. My work would consist of organising the small group of civilian staff who were there to service the vehicles and other general duties. My working hours were 09.00hrs until 16.00hrs, Monday to Friday. Also I had to be on hand on Tuesday and Thursday evenings which were drill nights for the TA members and as things stood at that time, I had to be present on Sundays to attend the Guidon rehearsals at Fenham Barracks as the RSM's assistant. This would take up all my Sundays until the event. I suppose my little perk was that I had Wednesday afternoon off.

LAST MAN STANDING

The preparation for the Guidon Parade began on two nights a week in the TA centre, indoors with foot drill and arms drill, then on Sunday's rehearsal on the square at Fenham until July.

So, I was launched into my new job. I quickly learnt the civilian staff were a joy to be associated with. There were three other members of the military permanent staff, all together a very nice team. We also shared the TA centre with a small REME unit. Their PSI invited my RSM and I for a drink and snack in the REME Sergeants Mess. A very nice gesture and appreciated by both of us. Many experiences were aired and there was much laughter to be heard. Then there was a knock on the door, the barman went to open it to reveal the adjutant standing there. We all stood up and he informed us that he had been hunting high and low for us. I stood there waiting for someone to speak and thank the lord the RSM said "Can I get you a drink sir?" The adjutant replied, "I thought you were never going to ask". At that point it probably would seem in the CO's eyes as if the gathering was going downhill, but I doubt he would get to know. The situation in the REME mess had now progressed from a welcome get-together, to an in-depth top-level conference on the reparation for the Guidon Parade. Unnecessary, but on the other hand quite amusing and it brought people together. It's nice to get on with your neighbours and for the remainder of my time there that friendship and cooperation never diminished.

I was told by the RSM to look out for the

TA chaps who would possibly never make the grade through a lack of coordination and inherent inability to concentrate. Thank the lord there were only two of them and their removal was dealt with discreetly. This left me unhindered to concentrate on coaching the escort to the Guidon. This comprised of both foot and arms drill, most of which was carried out in the confines of the TA centre. I found this at times somewhat restricting but with a little thought was achievable. The best place to produce our best results would only be on the parade ground at Fenham Barracks, but unfortunately we only had the use of those facilities on a Sunday and that was also the day the majority of the TA chaps were available because of their civilian jobs. It was gratifying to see so many turn up week after week.

As I had been here for some time now, I shall try to elaborate a little more on my duties. Firstly, I collect the squadron mail from the orderly office and sort it into their respective pigeonholes, then read any mail for me. I then check with the civilian staff, to ascertain if all transport is road worthy and if not why? If a vehicle is broken down and LAD cannot rectify the problem, it will have to go the REME workshops at Killingworth asap. I would visit the RSM's office to hand in the previous days report. Then I'd work out the programme for the next drill night, sort out a date for a practice shoot on the mini range, or plan a map reading exercise for some new recruits, which is to be supervised by an SSM and two sergeants from the TA unit. I often had to drive to Catterick Garrison for stores and equipment.

LAST MAN STANDING

Now and then I would be accompanied by the RSM, but usually one of the civilian staff. I enjoyed that for they could do the driving, I could relax and when we got to Catterick then with my business concluded, I would tell the driver to go to the dining hall and I would go to the Sergeants mess. A drink, a chat and hopefully meet up with an old friend.

By this time, I feel that life should be more settled, but unfortunately it was far from that. It was more like having two jobs that would seem to be exerting far too much pressure on Betty and my relationship. Therefore, some form of a solution would need to be found. We were unhappy but still very much in love. So, at that point I had a meeting with the RSM to see if it was possible to reschedule my off-duty hours. This was quite easy to arrange and within two weeks Betty had a position in the fashion department of a large city centre store. This changed our mode of life almost in an instant and we could spend more time together. We were able to save more toward buying a house and we must not overlook we also have a wedding to arrange in the very near future. As I had rented a TV, we would stay at home and watch that. Soon the stress and our concerns disappeared. To say we were in seventh heaven would not be an exaggeration. She loved her job and I was throwing myself into the rehearsals for the Guidon parade, which by now was just a few weeks away. The RSM had allocated a TA Sergeant, who was a former 12th Lancer and knew his job and would keep me informed of the progress of the escorts drill development.

Most of my duties were rather mundane at this point, for everything training wise has been put aside to facilitate the Guidon Ceremony. Fortunately, once that was achieved, we would be able to return to the more un-glamorous side of military training along with preparations for the Regimental camp. There was a very busy year ahead for all of us and at the end of it, the squad would most likely think the first part was the worst with that RSM and his Drill Sergeant. My advice to those totally uninformed part-time warriors *(after the show is over and they are attending the buffet celebration with family and friends, receiving the "well done lads" pats on the back and handshakes)*, just remember that RSM and his Drill Sergeant who, if you have a doubt, always keeps his birth certificate in his wallet in case it is necessary to clarify his authenticity. But this was never a problem, for as their concentration increased so did their sense of pride. They felt smarter, straighter and taller. They were at this time representing the British Army, the best in the world and to those who often query the value and the need or benefits of drill, I hope this will enlighten them. When the chips are down, no one can do it better.

Back to home life and Betty's new employment. It would appear all was going very well. She was working with a girl who started at the same time and who she had met at the interview. They obviously worked well together. They, I have been told, were the first ones on the department floor each day and on several occasions, they would receive a reward for their counter dressing and would also help each other to ensure their make-up was perfection. Therefore, it was just a matter of time before it became obvious that they were an asset to the store. The fashions manager offered them the chance to model the latest fashion at the stores new seasons show. I must confess I was both astounded and impressed with their achievement and need I add very proud.

Returning to my side of this story. I had undertaken to do some research into the members of the unit, who included former regulars or national servicemen and those who had enrolled with no former military experience. My idea was to help assess their development and progress, so to be able to make judgement as to what job they were best qualified to do. After I had compiled my assessment report, I had a long meeting with the RSM to discuss my recommendations. The outcome of our meeting was both flattering and, in my eyes, amusing for he thanked me and much to my surprise he concluded with a well-known Geordie term of friendship 'Well Done Bonny Lad' (he had picked up the lingo since his arrival in Geordie land). I suppose I had better watch out or he would want me to sponsor him for Geordie citizenship.

At this point I shall digress for a while as I relate a story about that fine gentleman, our RSM. He was driving home in his land-rover one evening when he was involved in a road traffic accident and admitted to hospital for observation. I called in the following day to visit and while I was by his bed talking to him, I noticed a very timid looking young chap (another patient apparently) gently polishing an already highly polished pair of shoes. The RSM noticed I was looking at them and so informed me that they were his. He told the nice young man to put more effort into his work and asked him if he had told the cleaner when she comes in if she is only half cleaning the ward and that he will accompany the cleaner tomorrow when she does her rounds. Lesson – don't mess with RSM.

It was Sunday and as we were without the RSM. It fell to me to oversee the drill rehearsal at Fenham Barracks for which I had the assistance of one of the TA sergeants, who as it happens was a former 12th Lancer. The day went off very well and my colleague for the day claimed to have gained more knowledge of drill in three hours than he did in three years in the army. Very flattering, but he would most probably only have had drill instruction in his training days and not for a ceremonial occasion. So, preparations continued until the Sunday before the actual event when it would be a dress rehearsal for the following weekend. In the meantime, it had been decided by the powers that be to form all of the regiments armoured vehicles in an extended line at the rear of the escort for the Guidon and for this one-off occasion they be known as the Mounted Squadron. On the parade the Mounted Squadron will fall in on the order "crews front". Then on the command "escort for the Guidon will advance in review order", the mounted squadron would mount their vehicles as the escort are advancing the thirteen paces and halt, at which point the officer will receive the Guidon from the Duke of Northumberland. When all this had been completed, the regiment was to march through the city, where the Duke would take the salute. When the parade departs the barracks to march through the city, it would be followed by the armoured vehicles of the mounted squadron which, after the drive past, would return to the TA centre and transport was to be waiting to return them to the buffet and bar at Fenham. This was carried out and concluded to an almost perfect and can I say to a very large extent, successful endeavour.

To bring this chapter of my times to a close, a personal observation. I have always felt that the idea to bring in a mounted element was ill conceived, or at best badly timed and introduced, leaving no time for training and rehearsal. To get an extended line of vehicles to move forward at a low speed takes a tremendous amount of time and concentration and, as it appeared to me, many of the units drivers had enrolled in the TA to gain the skills to do this and may not yet have achieved that level of expertise. This said, it was a success and I think that because of all that had taken place in the last few weeks, I detected an air of "look at me I'm a soldier". Finally, a few words of praise for the RSM for creating a truly outstanding body of men who would give the regulars a run for their money.

As ever time moves on and within a week the RSM was out of hospital and back on duty. He asked me for my view of the dress rehearsal. I assured him that the chaps who were in the escort to the Guidon and attended in number one uniform, were inspected by myself and Sergeant TA. There were one or two small adjustments to be seen to. I had told them to hand their uniforms in to me on their return to the TA centre so that I could take them to the tailor for the necessary alterations. The men would have to collect them from me on the Thursday drill night. Other than that, I had no problems with the escort and asked if he'd had time to read my comments on the situation as regards the mounted squadron. His response was etched on his face, his lips moved but no sound emerged. I told him there was no need to turn the volume up, I am receiving your message most clearly. Being the man he was, he said "leave it to me". I saw him later that day and he said he had brought the matter to the CO's attention. There will be a mounted squadron which will remain static until ordered to move. That will be after the Guidon and escort has been marched off and the mounted squadron will follow as instructed. He then told me that I would be in control of the transport to return the crews to Fenham Barracks. After the RSM's intervention, life seemed to settle down for the following two weeks leading up to the Guidon parade. One more dress rehearsal then the following Sunday the real thing. To say it went off well would not give those TA boys the credit they deserved, for they were truly magnificent. As I was not directly involved, I was standing with Betty in the VIP enclosure. On the opposite side of me there was a very smartly dressed gentleman who informed me he was a retired colonel and had received an invitation from one of the officers. He said after the march off that had he not been informed; he would have believed the troops on parade were a regular regiment. I was so happy to assure him and others who were nearby, that there was only one regular soldier out there and that was the RSM. Later, on my return for the buffet, I was surprised by the reception I got from the TA chaps. The CO and many of the VIP guests, best of all my Betty, and last but not least the RSM who would write to our regiment to inform our CO not to look for a drill pig "I have one here when required and thank you for sending him". I believe his closing comment was referring to me and I thanked him for the kind and much appreciated references, but if he would recall it was he and his example which I learned so much from. If there were to be any accolades, they should be directed at him. May I say a Warrant Officer and a Gentleman. No longer with us, but I am sure you will be playing a prominent part in that parade ground in the sky. God Bless.

Life went back to normal routine, the wheels were in motion preparing for the units annual training camp and it was decided that I should attend a small arms refresher course at the School of Infantry situated at Hythe, Kent. This brought back some very vivid memories of my childhood days when I spent my school holidays with my aunt and uncle, almost a repeat of those days but I will be attending a different school on this occasion. There will be some who may wish to query the reason for sending me off just as the unit were about to go to camp, so for the benefit of the inquisitive, there was a vacancy for someone to learn the rudiments of the then new GPMG (general purpose machine gun) being introduced to replace the good old, but heavy, Bren gun. The new line will most probably be heavier if I know the war horse. So, with that in mind I left for Kent and the school of infantry. The outstanding feature, that is as far as I was concerned, was the glorious weather with most classes outdoors and we had a half day off on the Wednesday, so with two friends we went for a trip on the Romney Hythe and Dymchurch Railway. The course ended with a test, not in the least complicated and I hastily headed for home. As I had only been away for ten days, on arrival home I had three days free as the regiment would be gone for a fortnight, so I was on my own.

Taking advantage of this free time to meet Betty and her work friend we all went for dinner in the Eldon Grill. This turned out for me a mixture of both amusement and embarrassment. Let me explain. On that particular night Newcastle United were playing a floodlit football match and the Eldon was full with young men going to the game. I entered the hotel lounge between two gorgeous ladies attired in the very latest fashion. Both tall, one blonde the other brunette, and they did light the place up. On entering the room, the sound level dropped, and the silence was deafening. In a short time they all appeared to regain their composure. It was then that those two very provocative ladies decided to up the temperature by saying things like "I love a man in uniform" or "it's great to snuggle up to a gallant sergeant". At this point I was beginning to get more than a little hot under the collar. The football supporters were on their way out to go to the match and as they thinned out I decided to visit the toilet, only to be confronted by some of them who wanted to know where I got the ladies from, some saying I bet they're on at the Theatre Royal. The discussion was going on out into the street and some saying I bet they're dancers in a show, but two of them held back and asked me "Come on Serg, where are they from?" I could not resist the temptation and said that they were military policewomen. One of the lads said that's great, but some said, "What dressed like that?" So, I told them that they were plain clothes officers. They all had a good laugh and off they went to cheer on the Toon. When they had gone, the girls and I enjoyed a meal and the rest of the evening. There is an old saying that nothing good lasts forever and that was what those few days were to me and Betty.

It was an early start on the Sunday for the arrival of the regiment from their two weeks of military training. Now it was cleaning down vehicles, returning stores and weapons to the armoury, then when the vehicles have been refuelled, check for cleanliness and ensure they're all parked in their designated area. Finally, go to the office and write up your report to hand into the RSM in the morning, when it will kick off again, but hoping someone else will be there to do it next year. As one would expect, there would be a long list of repairs to both vehicles and equipment. If necessary, it is a case of seeing the QM to order replacements. At such times you were soon up to your neck in paperwork. I must confess there were times I cheated, for I took some of my work home. Betty was much more accomplished in that department than I could ever be, therefore

I say leave it to the expert. It worked.

Life at the TA centre went on as normal. I received a signal from Catterick informing me there was an GPMG waiting for collection, *"please make the pick-up asap and advise"*. I informed the RSM who decided to accompany me, and he let them know we would be there the next day. This we did and had a very enjoyable meal in the sergeants' mess and found a little time to socialise, but not too long. Then it was back to the TA centre, place the GPMG in the armoury, then home for dinner and TV. The next day I carried out my usual morning routine, gave my report to the RSM at the end and asked if there would be anything else he required me for. If not, then I'd go to my office and draft up a training programme for the GPMG with the first class for NCO's and the following week for the troops. I would allow more time for that class, as there will be more personnel to deal with and time is very limited in the evenings. Once the programme was completed, I spent some time in the armoury stripping and assembling the gun. The following day I placed an order on the notice board. I also informed everybody on first parade on Tuesday night, to always check the notice board for the day, time, date and information of who should attend and who the instructor will be, for the subject and this time it will be the GMPG with the PSI.

There is very little else of interest to mention in the otherwise mundane running of this very well organised TA unit. As this is not and was never indented to be a diary, I will draw a line under this part of the chapter.

LAST MAN STANDING

Time had moved on so swiftly, I suddenly realised that I only had another eighteen months to do in the army and would have to sit down with Betty for a discussion regarding our future. Should I sign on, or leave the army? This in many ways would be a life changing decision and the solution was only acceptable if both of us agreed. Well, we had our discussion and reviewed the situation from both sides. There was she with her new job and me not knowing what I could turn my hand to, other than soldiering. She suggested, how about a driving job? I suddenly found myself saying yes. So, it was decided that I would not extend my regular army service, but if possible, I would become a member of the TA unit. I therefore had the unenviable task of informing the RSM. However, he didn't look in the least surprised when I spoke to him, and said he knew it was coming. He had already spoken to my own regiments CO, who despite his disappointment advised that should I wish at any time in the future to return to the regiment, I would be welcomed and it would be arranged for me to retain my rank. He had concluded with thanks and praise for my work and dedication. The RSM then told me I would remain as the PSI until my discharge, so for the time being, just carry on.

Therefore, that was the moment my future life was decided by my sweet lady. I am sure there were occasions during the years that followed, when she regretted that decision. I was to become a Long-Distance Trucker and had a lot of time away from home. But the financial benefits were rewarding and would give us the home and life we wished for.

In a few weeks we were to be married. This was be a somewhat quiet occasion. Betty had chosen two bridesmaids, my young sister and a friend. I asked an old school friend to be my best man. The day of our big event was drawing closer, but there was no need for panic as everything required was in hand. Invitations to a small number of friends and family had been sent out and no elaborate wedding gown or wedding breakfast. Just two very much in love people starting from scratch, spending wisely, so to budget for their home and hopefully some children and above all a long, happy and healthy life.

Up until the date of our wedding, the 5th of July 1952, there is nothing outstanding to write about other than our forthcoming marriage.

As planned and dreamed of, the big day arrived. 11am at Byker Parish Church, and at last we were officially as one. We, our family and friends had some refreshments at my parents' home, after which the newly-weds left for a short break at Saltburn-by-the Sea. There were no hitches and it was so nice to be away from all the work and planning. The weather was fine, the hotel was friendly and comfortable, the food was exceptional and despite the fact we never told them that we were honeymooners, we received a glass of bubbly with "we won't tell a sole". We very much appreciated their discretion; they were obviously well practised in recognising their clientele.

Then all too soon it was over, and we were

Anniversary
celebration

Betty and I at home

Betty and I cutting the wedding cake at our wedding reception

heading for home and work. Betty could not wait
to show off her wedding ring to her friends at
work, but I was not so enthusiastic. I suppose
what was on my mind was trying to find some way
of contacting someone who could help with the
move to civvy street. I can't say it was good
to be back in harness, an old cavalryman's
expression. As I had only been away for a few
days it seemed as though I had never been gone,
and I was now more convinced than ever that
this sort of army life was not for me. It left
me feeling like a civilian in uniform. This is
not to imply that being a member of the TA is
in any way a waste of time, far from it, it is
just not for me. So, I would just have to tough
it out until my time was up with the army. In
the time I had still to do, I gathered all
the information available on the road haulage
companies. I needed to establish how much
knowledge and experience I would require, and
are there any training schools? I soon found
out you would stand a much better chance if you
were ex forces. Therefore, with each week that
passed my confidence grew stronger. There was
just one matter that both Betty and I thought
we should do. As a stop gap, we needed to find
some alternative accommodation, as opposed to
living in with her father. So, the search began
to find something suitable, in good condition
and at reasonable rent. We were lucky and found
a flat in Byker and so moved in.

I have now arrived at the end of
my regular army career, by activating the
remaining unclaimed furlough. I will not spend
any more time on the intricacies of terminating
my regular army service. I am sure had I been

leaving the 4th Hussars it would have been a much more emotional occasion but now my mindset was focussed elsewhere, so let's move on.

CHAPTER 7

Civvy Street

I had been given the opportunity to join a local haulage company on a trial for one month. If I proved successful, there would be a position with the firm and this would put me on the bottom rung of the ladder, but hopefully launch me on my new career.

The haulage company, my new employers, was a family business administered and owned by three brothers. They treat their employees with respect and if appropriate, praise. Although not having themselves served in the forces, they were very veteran orientated, and it was their policy that staff and drivers were always smart and polite. They were also family supportive with summer picnics and a Christmas Party for the children, as well as a Dinner Dance for the grown-ups at the Old Assembly Rooms in Newcastle. So, it would appear I had made a good decision, making Betty and I very happy.

I well recall my first day back in civilian employment. I was, as one would expect, a little apprehensive. So much time had elapsed since joining the army and perhaps I had lived a sort of cocooned or sheltered life, but on reflection the situation was completely different to my first time at work. Then I was a young boy, now I am a married man with a different perspective on life.

I was confident about my driving ability but not fully acquainted as to the loading and securing of a truck. That to me was a big concern. But once more good fortune came my way in the form of a truly good but modest man, a highly qualified trucker that I will refer to as Joe. He was a member of the Burma Star Association who became a very good friend and remained so until the very end. He was my mentor. God Bless You Joe, in that truck park in Heaven.

To commence my training, I was instructed to take an Atkinson Tractor Unit and 40ft trailer to a local flour mill and load it with 20 ton of flour in sacks. For this, I would be accompanied by the driver foreman. Obviously, a test of my knowledge and adaptability. The foreman stood on the loading dock with his note pad and when the loading was completed, I then had to rope and sheet the load ready for the road and return to the depot. There everything was closely checked for safety and that the documentation was correct. Then I needed to fuel up the vehicle for the journey to Hull the next day. I was asked if I would like to do that delivery, after which there was a return load to be collected from a warehouse in Hull back for delivery to our depot. As I only had 8 hours driving time, I may not get home that evening but on that occasion, all went well for I had no hold-ups at Hull, so all in all a very good day.

The following day was spent in the depot. One of the brothers called me into the office to tell me that of my work so far, they were all

well pleased and impressed with my performance.
If I wished, they would be happy to cancel the
probation period. I could not wait to go home
and let Betty know. At work I remained in the
depot, to give me time to acquaint myself with
the various types of vehicles in the fleet.
Several of the articulated trucks had different
couplings, Scammel or Fifth wheel. There was
also a selection of trailers from flats of various
lengths to low loaders. As this illustrates,
this was a very comprehensive haulage company
and it would seem they do not try and force the
pace with new employees. They help them settle
into the company's standards and objectives.
This policy appeared to produce the desired
effect for the employers were happy, as were
the employees and I am sure the customers
appreciated the service they received from the
staff and drivers.

I was grateful for the way I had been helped
by the depot staff and drivers, particularly my
new friend Joe, with a wealth of good advice.
Joe had worked there for a good number of years
and was somewhat older than me, but I always
felt comfortable in his presence. Perhaps it
went back to our service days when we both,
at different periods of time, were engaged in
jungle warfare which created a natural bond.

Life was settling into a calmer mode,
Betty was very contented with her position
at work, I was learning more and more each
day, and everyone was so helpful. Perhaps this
atmosphere was created because everyone knew
their classification and wage scale, which was
based on the class of vehicle they drove. There

was a company savings scheme whereby you could have a set sum withdrawn from your salary to enhance your holiday pay. You were also issued with two pairs of work overalls, one set could be handed in for washing each week, the cost of which was covered by the company. Therefore, no excuse for a less than tidy turnout.

So much for how this organisation operated; smart, pleasant and efficient.

As a new week began. I was allocated a full week's work schedule, which is not unusual as much of the contract work was planned in that manner. Apparently, it was much easier to rotate this sort of work so that the drivers do not get bored doing the same job or journey week in and week out. There were several drivers who preferred to do what in the trade is referred to as tramping. This would comprise of loading out over, then picking up a return load as directed, to wherever. This often required you being away for most of the week.

My first contract job would involve loading 20 ton of flour at a local mill to deliver to a bakery in Aspatria, Cumbria. Then when unloaded, go to Whitehaven Products and load with soap powder to be delivered to the Co-op soap works at Irlam, Manchester. Once unloaded, then reload with soap to be transported to our home depot for local branch delivery. This resulted in two nights away from home and I would continue this for the rest of the week which resulted in a repeat journey. On my return to the depot with load discharged, I was told I would be doing the same run next week. So, it was off to home and Betty for I hoped, a nice weekend.

As for the past week and the one ahead, for me I did not find it too difficult and enjoyed driving through the Lake District with all its beautiful landscape. What a contrast from the boring drab motorways we so often travel on. One wondered where I would be sent after the next week.

A leap forward two weeks, and I would find myself heading for Southampton to exchange a loaded 40ft container for an empty one to be returned to our depot.

From this point I will only refer to where I am going and any incident that may occur along the way. So, I was on my way to southeast London and then to Basingstoke to collect and deliver a sea container to TVTE (Team Valley Trading Estate) in Gateshead. This was my daily routine and all that could be different would be the type of load or its destination. So, in fact it was, shall I say, quite uneventful much of the time.

A few years after I'd became established as a long-distance trucker, newer vehicles and designs were taking to the road, with features such as sleeper cabs. A great advantage to both the company and the drivers. Regarding driver comfort and welfare, I think the haulage industry had a lot of catching up to do. I do not wish to malign anybody and I can only base my view on what I was told by the older drivers I met after initially becoming a member of this illustrious body, who gave me an insight into the sort of accommodation that was available between the 1950s until the introduction of the sleeper cab.

So, moving on and good news was on its way, for Betty informed me that I was going to be a father. I first thought "my god more responsibility" but also much more joy. A new baby, perhaps a baby girl as beautiful as her mother, or it may be a boy who would grow up to be a train driver, a ship's captain or a famous footballer. But on the other hand, I would not mind as long as they were healthy, honest and a credit to the family. Betty's response to my daydreaming "it will more than likely be a girl, so what would you have in mind for her?" If I recall correctly, I am sure I said a train driver. I think she responded by saying "don't be cupid", but she said later it was "stupid". My reply to that was "you married me". For some reason her response consisted of two words, I could not identify the first, but could not mistake the second was definitely "off".

So, it was off to work in the knowledge I would soon be a dad. When Betty began to show, she was put on maternity leave. I changed from day shift to night shift until a week before the baby was due, that being about the end of January.

Work continued in its normal way with a variety of destinations such as the usual list of airports Heathrow, Gatwick (or as we call it Grassport Airwick), East Midlands, Stansted and other smaller ones. As you would gather from

David Jnr. Seeing Dad off to work

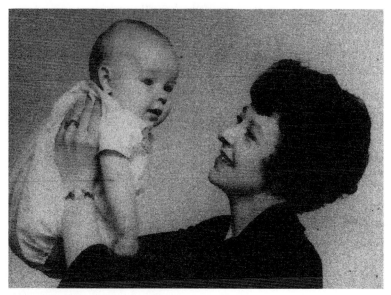

Betty with baby David 4 months old

Betty relaxing in the garden in Tidiworth

these and the seaports, work was plentiful and consistent therefore no problems financially. Betty was in good shape (a play on words) and I now knew I was to be the father of a boy, so at that time I don't think life could have been better. By then we had our home decorated and furnished, happiness is Betty shaped and our lives were full of love.

I had every reason to be happy. The traffic manager, with the approval of all the other drivers, gave me the loads that were of a short duration so for the moment I was home each night.

It seemed no time at all that the new arrival would be putting in his first appearance being due on the 24th January. Much like his father, he arrived bang on time 4:00pm on the 24th of January, weighing in at 10 pounds. Mother a little worse for wear. On my arrival at the maternity ward I was confronted by the ward sister demanding to know what I had been feeding her on "we had to bring in her doctor to bring this fine young man into the world and oh that noise is her". She pointed to the door opposite and I asked if it was alright for me to go in. The sister said, "oh yes, she isn't violent just noisy'". However, when I entered she had fallen asleep so I thought I would sit there until she woke up. Well, an hour later the sister came by and saw me and asked, "are you still here?". Obviously, the reply was yes, and she told me she had given Betty something to sleep. My new son was also fast asleep and so off I went to have a meal and I hoped a good night's sleep, perhaps even a pleasant dream or two.

I had arranged with my employers to take some leave to be with Betty when she came home with baby. Taking that two-week holiday break was wonderful, from bringing baby home and the thrill we both experienced at starting our own little family. I still recall Betty saying, "well pop you got your wish, your son. So, let's hope he fulfils your dreams and perhaps in a year or two I will get my wish". My reply of "Do we have to wait that long?" I am not too certain of the exact phrasing of her reply, but I am sure it was somewhat unflattering. On reflection it was most probably an inappropriate suggestion at that point in time.

Casting my mind back to that period of my life it appeared to me in so many ways a much more relaxed mode of life. Considering we had survived the war and were coming out of rationing, cinemas were thriving, there was the NHS to attend to our health needs and all the dance halls were full every evening. There was also the Wednesday afternoon tea dance at the Oxford Galleries. New ships were under construction in the shipbuilding yards the length of the Tyne. Coal mines were in full production in the North East coal fields and the last of the war time servicemen were returning home. To top it all we had a new Queen on the throne. But my oh my, look at us now.

Those two weeks went by so very quickly. I find this is always the case when one is enjoying oneself. Helping to let Betty have some rest, fortunately the little cherub was no bother at nights and even if I say it myself, I was becoming quite proficient at preparing baby's bottle. What a contrast to my normal life as a soldier, then trucker. I sensed that I was going to enjoy parenthood.

During this time Betty's aunt looked after baby, so we could go together to purchase a pram. As Betty was quite tall, she wanted a large one and those who knew her will know what I am implying. It outshone the Queens Rolls. She would have it in mind that it should look as close as possible to whatever she was wearing. I always thought I had won the hand of the fairest maiden, and I had. The pram was soon delivered and that was the signal to fire the starting pistol to begin promenading up and down Shields Road and Heaton Park with baby in his designer pram, propelled by his suitably attired mother. To this very day I feel a sense of pride just thinking of her.

Things were going well; After several long discussions, for there had been a lot of suggestions on what to name the baby, we decided on David Matthew. David after myself and Matthew after Betty's father. The christening would be held at my local church St John the Evangelist in Wallsend. We were both happy and young David was developing into a fine and healthy boy and life to me was wonderful.

My paternity leave (as I'll call it, albeit this was long before such leave existed), was ending and I would have to return to work. There were no worries however, as Betty was in good health and I had to earn what was needed to maintain our quality of life. So, I contacted the company and was advised to start on the Monday doing some work in the depot for a start, then I would go back to my usual work the following week. So, I returned and did a variety of jobs shunting, transhipping loads and occasionally driving a fork-lift truck. There appeared to be abundance of work, which was not surprising in the least, for this company had an outstanding reputation for service and safety.

I had returned to work but worryingly I began to realise that I needed to increase my income to compensate for Betty's loss of earnings and the expense of bringing up baby. Up to that time I had been content, but my concern was in terms of how many hours I needed to work doing what I was doing, to get somewhere near the money I could earn if I were to go back on to long-distance work. It was a dilemma, which way should I go? I could ask Betty to spin a coin to decide, then I stopped short. Is there somewhere inside me a coward who would let his wife take the decision. No, the simple answer was for me to decide and hope for her approval. Well needless to say, her approval was forthcoming. She was aware of the predicament and was fully aware of our potential cashflow situation. She had the confidence in me to see us through the current problem. With that sort of trust and support, I knew our love would never fail.

As I sit at my desk writing this, I am feeling so very vulnerable emotionally, I am completely overwhelmed and will have to pause to avoid a tear or two dropping on this page, perhaps it is time for composure and coffee.

To the reader I apologies for that digression, it was unavoidable for I loved her with every fibre of my being and always will.

After I had been with my first haulage company for a couple of years, offers and opportunities with other transport operators began to come my way. Inevitably perhaps, I did therefore make several moves between employers over time. I had to do what was best for Betty, me and our lives. So, where opportunities for better pay and quality of work became available, I had to take what was best for us. After several years and a couple of jobs went by, I was made a particularly attractive offer that was too good to refuse. The attractiveness in financial terms was however offset to a degree in that there was an element of personal risk associated with this job. At times I would be required to transport what are classed as vulnerable loads that could attract unwanted interest by the wrong elements. I won't expand on this any further, for I must consider that although I am retired and out of that life, there are still those out there doing the same job and taking similar risks today. They don't claim to be supermen or latter-day heroes, just a trucker doing their job by day and night. I am proud to have had the opportunity to be counted in their ranks.

I had therefore now moved on to this pasture new, and for me this is where the fun began. My new colleagues were the most hilarious bunch I have ever encountered in my life both in and out of the army.

To get to know the job I did one trip from Tyneside to Heathrow and return. I quickly picked up the security aspect of this extremely vital work. What I can say, it involved continuous communications throughout the time the cargo is in the drivers care. This would be at times spent waiting at a seaport or an airport cargo terminal, be it for discharge or collection. It needs emphasised that the hauliers involved in this class of work made every effort to satisfy customers requirements. In line with this, they expected their drivers to display this in their efficiency and ethics and helps explain the personal terms and conditions that attracted me to the job. They were appropriate in the requirement for and recognition of driver loyalty and dedication.

I will avoid more repetitive non-descriptions of motorway journeys with very little to pass comment on, other than the weather and the amazing number of bad drivers. On the subject of the weather I have on many occasions travelled from, say Dover or Southampton, back to the north east and driven through perhaps five changes of weather in a distance of less than four hundred miles. Somewhat different to driving in say parts of continental Europe, where one can pass through three countries and the climate will be unchanged throughout.

I will now come to a point where I hope I can put a few smiles on the readers face. You may recall earlier I emphasised the humour of my new workmates. On many occasions we were required to travel in convoy. Our vehicles were equipped with two-way radios that connected us to an intercontinental security network. I shall refer to a colleague by initials or pseudonym, as I have no wish to risk embarrassing or offending valued friends. So here I go. Among the drivers was H, a good driver and a very witty chap who because of his laid-back attitude, always appeared to lag behind the rest of our convoy. When he complained that the rest of us kept leaving him, we would respond by saying he was too slow. On one occasion when we were ribbing about his speed, or lack of it, his retort was quick and amusing. He told us he had had a dream; it was the Battle of Britain. He was a Spitfire Pilot and as such had the power and talent to overtake anything, so with great bravado got onto the tail of an ME109, his challenge was to shoot it down but realised he had overtaken it and he got shot down by his target.

After H, I will continue with how I see the others. That would have to be GG, the drivers' union rep. A very nice chap. He was in appearance not unlike a popular popstar of the 70's and had to contend with a lot of leg-pulling from all his workmates. But I think he was happy to get his revenge, by the level of attention he received from the young ladies in the offices and service areas.

Next on my list would have to be Dodger, an admirer of all things female, in his own mind a Casanova, who I shall return to shortly.

I shall introduce my next mate, who resides with his partner in an old but rather quaint little cottage, which had in the past been the residence of a gatekeeper of a level crossing on a now defunct railway. A wonderful fellow and a charming partner. The gatehouse was somewhere near the highest point in County Durham.

Please do not think I am being disrespectful, as that is not something I would be to my former colleagues or truckers anywhere. They're a unique collection of professionals who ply their trade on the nation's roads by day and by night, the lifeline of the nation. Pardon me for that digression I will return to the pen portraits of my colleagues.

As promised earlier, I will give a brief description of the aforementioned Dodger. Please don't ask me who thought that name up, it was in existence when I arrived. I think he had some problems of which I know nothing. He was a nice chap, but always on the lookout for more money. Perhaps therein may lie the answer.

Although I may have been classed as the new kid on the block, they all would want me to make my own contribution. So, on that premise I will recollect here my effort. A convoy of 5 vehicles left our depot bound for Gatwick Airport in the following order of march. In front was me ZG1, then Dodger ZG2, and in the rear was H with his reputation for getting lost. But we have a way of dealing with that.

Some readers may be a little mystified as

to why I would be in the lead as a new driver. Well it just happened I was the first to arrive at the loading point and there is no stipulated order of march and no one objected. When we were all prepared, we moved off. Our first rest halt was at Micklefield, Yorkshire. The stop was for 45 minutes and the security guards looked after the vehicles. GG realised he had not handed in his time sheet for the previous week and everyone told him to phone it in from here. This he did and was on the phone a considerable time. When he eventually came back, he had been given some instructions from the traffic manager regarding return loads after we had discharged the present cargo's at Gatwick. There was much rejoicing at this news, as it would mean more money. GG read out the message that two vehicles load empty pallets at Gatwick to be returned to Gateshead and two vehicles would go to Wookey Hole in Somerset to load paper to transport to the north east. Oh, good grief! How sad, 4 loads and there are 5 trucks, someone is out of luck. But no, as GG our union rep will make the judgement of Solomon. Hooray, GG has the answer. Short straw will return home empty (for straw read matchstick). I am sitting thinking this is as good a time as any to make my mark, so I intervened by declaring I don't wish to take part so work it out between the four of you. The cry went up from all of them "no Dave, you are one of us now we must be fair". I still declined, there were pats on the back and "you're a good n Dave, I knew when you joined us" and compliments of that ilk.

As it was time to move, we set off in the direction of the M1 our next stop Watford

Gap. Driving the leading vehicle gave me the opportunity to fine tune my plan. The guard accompanying me was also an ex-serviceman. As mentioned, we were all in radio contact only achievable if operating on the same wavelength. These radios have two channels and we operated on channel A. Channel B is a spare, open but not in use. After some research I found I could, if I wish, use it. So, this was the perfect opportunity to activate my wind up. I told my companion guard and he was all for it. When we joined the M1, I switched to channel B and called Help Northampton to call Zulu Gray 1 on channel A and inform him to return to base after unloading at Gatwick as the Amsterdam job is on. Oh dear, behind me there was much flashing of headlights and sounding of horns. Then on arrival at Gatwick much running about looking for telephones and for the life of me I don't know why shouting something about a bar steward! Result a total success, outcome acceptance based on the premise that I was barmier than them. Shall I say, here endeth the first lesson.

By an amazing coincidence I and one of my workmates bumped into my former officer while having a rest break at a service station in Kent. Who should it be, non-other than Cpt K, my boss from my Malaysia days. He was getting out of his car as we were returning to our trucks. I did not notice him at first then I heard someone say, "good grief it's Sergeant Neil". He was in full dress uniform. He had his wife with him, and I quipped "you didn't have to dress up just to meet me". We all had a chuckle and he introduced me to his new wife, and I introduced my work colleague come friend. I inquired as to why he was in full dress and he explained that they were on their way to a passing out parade at Didcot. Being K, he asked my friend what I was like to work with, to which he replied, "as mad as a march hare". K replied, "oh, he hasn't got any better then?" and my colleague responded "if he has, it looks as if he must have been bloody awful when you had him and I'm sure the enemy saw him in a much different light". Time was moving on and both parties had to complete their respective journeys, leaving me now with regret, for I would not get to meet him again, I was informed sometime after this meeting, that he had passed away, the sad news coming in a letter from his wife. I was most grateful in my response to her. The burial was held in Somerset, attended by regimental officers. God Bless, we will all meet in the appropriate place at the appointed time. Ment et Manu, on behalf of the Band of Brothers. The one we all considered to be immortal has gone, but we are hopefully all better because of his example of courage and loyalty. I am sure this short epitaph will be met with approval by his old troop.

Ever since that chance meeting with K, I became aware of a change in my relationship with my workmates. Up to that time they all knew I was ex-service but little or nothing of my past. It would appear my colleague who was with me when I met K, had relayed the story of our meeting to the rest of the drivers and as inevitably happens, it began to lose its authenticity. Therefore, on several occasions I would have to correct some of my friends who had been misinformed or misquoted. In all honesty, it was at times rather flattering, but also could be embarrassing. I just had to make them understand I was not a hero, not at any time. I had been a soldier no more, no less. Before I made it clear to my workmates, I had a word with GG and asked him to give me some back up. This he did in his capacity as union representative but did add that I was maybe being just a little over shy. I was by now getting rather frustrated and asked not to be treated like a hero. I think it had finally got through to him and in time the others too. Hero no, soldier yes. And proud to have served my Queen and country.

Business carried on as normal but there was something different. At the risk of sounding arrogant, but definitely not meaning to be (as in my mind it is a recipe to attract hostility or dislike so I discourage that line of thought), it was nice for some to treat you with respect, or even seek your advice and thereby show trust and reliability. But that is as far as it needed to go and anything more was never what I wanted or desired. I just hoped not to have to navigate an awkward road of this nature again.

Well it was back to the highways and byways to earn, but it was a good start for me as the gaffer had put me on the Salford Sea Container run, one down and one back every day. As it happens it was a well-paid job and if I didn't encounter any delays or other hold-ups, I could be home every night. I thought if I were to speak to the Traffic Manager, I hoped it could be arranged for me to stay on the run.

LAST MAN STANDING

This I did and spoke to the boss who had no objection, but I would have to put this to the union rep, GG, and after some consultation with the drivers, they gave the idea their blessing.

Thank goodness the situation looked really good. All being well my income for the immediate time had the potential of some consistency, which is a great help for any forward planning we may wish to undertake. So, let me say I now had an air of confidence and the feel-good factor was fully functional.

Therefore, let it be *"wagons roll, 10-4"*.

I was so pleased that good fortune had come my way once more for it appeared that I was in the right place at the right time to land a plumb job like this, with a good chance of being home each night and be with my wife and baby. I can't think of a better situation for a trucker to be in.

I set out at 8:00am Monday morning for my first trip and as I turned onto the M62 at Ferrybridge the thought crossed my mind *"how long will it be before I get bored with the same journey every working day?"* Well, so as not to drag this episode out I shall tell you now, a total of 13 years and it only came to an end by me doing someone a good turn. In my mind it was probably the happiest days of my time as a trucker and yes, it was as you may imagine, a painful parting and I can assure you that was not an understatement for by fulfilling this favour I ended up with a 4ton steel section falling on my left leg almost severing my left

103

foot. You will see that my previous remarks were a play on words, but sad to say this is where my sense of humour abandons me.

The reader may find it rather puzzling as to why I took a huge leap forward in time at this point. Let me explain, in my own perception this is a chronicle of events that have occurred in my life and I am attempting to maintain the continuity by stepping over a most disinteresting and repetitive period of my life as a trucker and working on the assumption that in all probability you would drop off to sleep or bin the book, but I am sure if you continue, I hope you will feel you made the right choice. So, let us return to the story.

My quite horrific injury as sustained due to an inadequate loading procedure that in my opinion, used inappropriate lifting equipment and a less than competent operator. With my occasional good luck, a former army officer I had served under and who was by then a solicitor, came to my assistance and fortunately got things settled without me having to attend court.

During the time which has elapsed from the accident, the injury has restricted my mobility, even to this day, a period of some forty plus years.

I am sure the reader would in all probability have no great desire for me to dwell on my ordeal of pain and discomfort, but I am sure I would be remiss in not paying tribute and thanks to the doctors and nursing staff at the Queen Elizabeth Hospital in Gateshead for the wonderful care I received. And above all, to an outstanding surgeon who performed a very difficult operation to save me having my left foot amputated. He is probably no longer with us by now but bless you sir and a thousand thanks.

As you may realise, I could not return to work for a considerable length of time. If that surgeon was a hero, then there was also a heroine. Yes, my wife Betty. Can you imagine, a young wife and mother with limited help, me hobbling about the house and to a large extent having to rely on friends or workmates to support with shopping and various other chores.

Then one day we received a phone call from the Traffic Manager to ask if the company MD could call to have a chat with me. What could I do, other than to say yes? When I told Betty, she came over to my chair gave me a kiss, knelt, held my hand and assured me that together we would see this through. My confidence was completely restored. I was then prepared to respond with some dignity, when he delivers the poisoned chalice *("sorry we can no longer employ you… etc")*. I had never seen or spoken to the man. Good grief I was completely astounded. When Betty brought him into the lounge, she was holding some flowers and he a bottle of rum. We exchanged the customary niceties and Betty suggested he may care for some refreshment, he said coffee black no sugar. There I was witnessing all this, and he is about to fire me. Well, in fact he is not. My overactive imagination had, I admit, gone into overdrive. I found myself quite humbled for this very understanding gentleman to visit my wife and me, with the main purpose to reassure us both that come what may as the result of my injuries, they would find a position for me within the company. To say I was very impressed would be a gross understatement. I was totally gob-smacked. When I had recovered my composer, I told him that this had not been what I was expecting, and I was having to try and get my mind around this. He told me the drivers had been concerned and among them collected a sum of money which he handed to me in package. There was £500.

It was a great surprise but most welcome news from the MD that my position with the company was secure and when I asked him to pass on my thanks to my work mates his response was "you mean the wild bunch". He then went on to explain that it all began when GG organised a meeting of the drivers and the two-warehouse staff, but it appears that the initiative of the drivers went into overdrive. They persuaded the owner and staff to place a notice about my misfortune along with a collection box beside the till asking for donations. The outcome was so impressive and very much appreciated by me and Betty. As I said earlier, truckers are a brotherhood and therein lies the support I received. I sincerely hope the reader will bear in mind when they are next overtaking one of those juggernauts, the person behind the wheel is just someone out there earning a living and more often than not making a delivery of something that may end up in your home. So please remember, he or she are on the move day or night throughout the changing seasons, be it food, fuel and so many other commodities, to make our lives liveable. There may be some who feel my observation perhaps is a little over emphasised. That is their prerogative, perhaps brought about by a bad experience at some time whilst driving, and I would be the first to concede to their opinion. There will always be the odd one or two drivers who are by a country mile an exception to the norm, but please give them some room to do their very responsible work.

As I was now wheelchair bound and still uncertain if I would ever be able to walk unaided again, I was collected and transported to and from hospital twice a week and a district nurse visited on alternate days to change my dressings. This was working out quite well up to and until I had to have another x-ray when the consultant was unhappy about the swelling in the area of the fracture and immediately stopped the physiotherapy. He, I feel, had the look of someone who had been let down. I was taken to x-ray after which I was returned to the consulting room. He immediately viewed the result and after some deliberation said, "well young man, I regret to tell you that another operation is required as you are going to need a bone graft". This would mean taking some bone from another part of my body for the graft. Just as I was beginning to feel comfortable and a little more relaxed, I was left with a feeling of despair and frustration. If I have any luck it appears to be cancelled itself out right now.

I was admitted to Tynemouth Jubilee

hospital the following week on the Monday and had the operation the next day. I was discharged the following Tuesday with strict orders under no circumstances was I allowed to walk for at least two weeks. At that time, I would be x-rayed once more and then wait for the consultant's verdict and decision. I was told that I could go home now by the hospital transport and I would get a letter from the consultant regarding my future treatment. In the meantime, I would continue with my physio treatment twice a week. Hospital transport was arranged and so home I went to wait for the next move. I suddenly realised on my journey home, a feeling which I can't recall having before. It was a combination of joy, comfort and love for at the end of that journey was my beautiful wife and my young boy, in our cosy little home surrounded by all I love. As things worked out, we could manage in some comfort, so happy and so in love. I perceived an even brighter future yet to come. I hope something nice will take place.

Well before not too long something nice really did, when the doctor confirmed that Betty was pregnant. I could not describe the feeling that radiated from us. I was thinking, what were the words? Joy, thrilled, laughter, excitement, anticipation, but mainly love.

Eventually I regained my composure, it was time for baby talk. It was a little early to be sure if it would be a girl or a boy and it was unwise to rush out and purchase clothing until we knew one way or the other. I said it may be twins and she replied, "and

Me as a trucker

Me with Tony and Dennis, wagons roll.

Betty and friend in London

may be dead". With that I immediately withdrew from the conversation and made a cup of tea. I brought Betty's tea in for her and she said she was sorry, but it's a women thing. It was after her next clinic they confirmed that it was a baby girl and David junior had a little sister. I wondered if I would be back to work when she arrives or still at home to give some help to Betty in what is a very busy time. But that time is, for my way of thinking, still a long way off.

It was at this point in my recovery that I began to fully understand the gravity of the injury I had sustained in that accident. I found it difficult to find forgiveness in my heart, but I must.

I had now reached a stage where I was at a crossroad in my recovery, leaving me with a wish to move on with more haste. I needed the medical team to give me some idea as to how long it would be before they could make a decision regarding my future. They had already reduced my physiotherapy sessions and the district nurse had discontinued her visits. Surely that was an indication that a great amount of progress had been achieved. My natural assumption was that it would be very near for a decision to be forthcoming, but when I brought the matter to the family GP, he told me not to rush my recovery. "To a layman they think they know, but to the professional they do know and if you undo the outstanding job of the surgeon and his team, both you and others will never forgive yourselves". So, as an old soldier I bit on the bullet and obeyed.

Therefore, after being rebuked by my GP for, as he put it, "a lack of moral fibre", it now became clear to me that I was pursuing the wrong approach to a full recovery. His advice was in the form of a most ego deflating comment that anyone could have directed at them. I am not unfamiliar with the expression, I'd heard several times before, but that was during my army days and, I must emphasise, never directed at me.

I just had to knuckle down and concentrate on my exercise programme. It was then decided that it would be beneficial to fit me with a leg calliper, to give the area of the bone graft some additional support and help me towards an earlier return to work. This did not guarantee it would make the healing any quicker, but it would not slow it down. One thing it did, was give me more confidence while attempting to revive my mobility to something near to normal. So, with the combination of this guidance and the previous assurance from the MD, why should I worry? Other than my hospital appointments, I had little to do other than wash up, peel potatoes and keep David entertained. There would now be short walks and when I could, I would accompany Betty shopping. On very special occasions Betty's cousin would baby sit leaving us to enjoy some free time on our own. Now and then we would dine out or just go for a drink and a chat. We were just happy in our own company and so very much in love. I now can see how we survived those painful years. So, life had to go on and the weeks and months flew by. The longer this went on the more I didn't want to return to my old job. For quite some time I concealed my feelings from Betty and my workmates when they visited me. Like so many occasions throughout my life, something will occur to help and how right I was. After a considerable period, my wonder woman gave me the solution to my dilemma. That was when she said, "I wish you were still at the TA Centre and be home every night". It took some time to absorb her comment, for it was then it dawned on me that she too had been concealing her feelings. This to me was heaven. We just sat there hugging each other. My mind was made up, I would contact the RSM next day to see if there was any work and try to put an end to what had been bothering me for the last few weeks.

When I told her I just could not face leaving her and now the children week after week, I had the incentive to achieve our goal and did not want to go back to my old job, she came over and hugged me then said "that is two brilliant things you have decided". My response was "not going away again is one what is the other?" "Marriage!" she exclaimed, then adding we must have had the longest courtship on record, four years.

So, for the rest of that evening we discussed our future and our in-transit daughter Fiona. The outcome was the realisation we would require a larger house sometime soon.

It was shortly after this I was contacted by the RSM at the TA centre to enquire if I would be interested in returning to my former position with the unit. There are those who may be a little confused at this, so let me explain.

I withdrew from the civilian employment, but I was still an active member. Because of my current injuries, I had been compelled to take no part in active involvement. Up to this time I had not bothered them and they me, so I visited the RSM the following day at the TA centre and had a chat with my old friend and comrade. He remarked on my leg calliper saying, "I see your leg is armoured, will you only re-join when you have gone Full Metal Jacket?". I replied, "if you can reinstate me perhaps the LAD can do the job, or the REME workshop at Killingworth".

Our conversation continued and he told me that my position had not been filled as he had undertaken to handle the office work which, he confessed, was banking up on his desk. He would have a word with the CO who, he was sure, would sanction my previous position at the TA Centre.

I suggested that it would be in my mind, the right and good-mannered way to bring about the termination to my civilian employment, quoting my lack of full fitness and my regret that I had to make this decision. I'd thank them all for their support and kindness and give them an assurance that the company and staff were in no way involved in my accident. The perpetrator was an employee of a customer, and my own solicitor had dealt with this matter to my satisfaction. It was not an easy decision to make, but I had to take into consideration the family factor, my wife and two young children. And that is apart from my own physical condition, which hopefully would improve over time.

It may appear to some that I had opted for

the soft option. Quite the opposite however, for I would be a little worse off financially. But with the knowledge of how Betty and I planned and worked together. we were convinced we had made the right decision.

Therefore, it was time to return to active involvement at the TA Centre.

CHAPTER 8

Back In Khaki

So, a new chapter in my life begins with me sitting behind a desk wading through a mountain of paperwork to be filed or replied to. This was the RSM's kind and thoughtful gesture, his idea of light duties. I did ask him if there would be an incentive to do a job I was not trained for, his reply was "good, you see your training now". He made us both a cup of tea, disregarding the last comments, for he was just creating a platform to allow me to ease myself back into work.

It was in the early weeks of my return to work that the RSM suggested that it was not necessary for me to attend the centre on drill nights or weekends and delay my return to full duty, until I can dispense with the leg calliper. He said he did not want to see the drill sergeant parading about the centre doing a sub-standard impression of Long John Silver, "it's bad for discipline". Good old Tom, he never had a sense of humour until he came to live in Geordie land.

I was fortunate to have a former comrade such as Tom to guide me through this thought challenging journey from my army life to what was almost a civilian life. But not quite, as to me it was a virtual minefield, but with his help and advice it was a stroll in the park.

LAST MAN STANDING

And meantime at home things were going to plan. That was my darling Betty's silhouette was undergoing something of a change. It would appear out little girl is getting bigger every day, so it won't be long now. We were reassured that there appeared to be no complications, thank the lord for that. I felt that we'd had more than our share of problems. I hoped that we could move on from here.

The work I inherited from the RSM's in-tray by now was evaporating, leaving me some free time. This gave me an opportunity to make use of some PE equipment in the miniature range, the idea being to speed up my recovery and become more active, hopefully helping to increase my return to full fitness. I was hoping to achieve the required standard to take part in putting the new recruits over the assault course.

Shortly after I initiated my own personal training programme, I arrived home one evening and Betty advised me that there was a letter from the hospital. This instructed me to attend an appointment the following week, for a full assessment. The letter went on to say that it may take a considerable time and could involve x-rays. Betty and I discussed the situation and concluded that we would just hope nothing untoward would crop-up, hopefully meaning that I could come home with some good news. It prompted me to think back over the years and recall, as told earlier in an earlier chapter, the time when I was very young and suffered a life-threatening accident which through a combination of good luck and care I survived.

At the time of writing, I'm here thinking how perhaps I was I born under a lucky star. There's plenty happened to suggest that the case or theory of this has certainly been put to the test it would seem.

So now was the time to hope and wait, exercise one's ability to remain calm and composed. If the decision is not to your liking, try once more.

Well the day of the appointment quickly arrived. I see no point in making a meal of this, we had waited so long. Fit for Duty! As is almost inevitable, a cautionary note however and that was to not over stretch myself for the first few weeks. I was also handed a copy of the report to give to the regimental medical officer.

I returned to the TA Centre and reported to the RSM who was delighted with the news and as it was a Thursday afternoon gave me the remainder of the week off. He said that we would have a planning meeting on Monday. I was somewhat puzzled as to the purpose, but he went on to tell me that the annual camp this year had been brought forward, so naturally everything would need to be arranged to comply to the requirements for the camp.

The meeting the following Monday was convened, which comprised of the Adjutant, QM, RSM and me. It commenced with the usual formalities, then the RSM introduced the new Adjutant. Once the meeting was opened by the Adjutant, it became clear the reason for this

118

hastily required gathering. This was to brief the regiment of their designated role in a three-day counter insurgency and this will involve the full Brigade. When he announced this, he had a smile on his face and commented "it would be interesting to know what was going on in the minds of the RSM and Sergeant Neil. It didn't escape my attention, the exchange of glances between them when I revealed the object of the exercise. For the benefit of those present who are not aware of their pedigree, you are in the company of two extremely, may I say, talented solders, who I hope can help us achieve some accolades at the end of the exercise". At the end of his report he asked if there were any questions. At this point the RSM thanked the Adjutant on behalf of himself and me. He then went on to inform all present that on the occasion of this year's Annual Camp, Sgt Neil may not be available, for although he now thinks he is fit, I have known him too long to be fooled, we should wait and see.

The meeting closed and I returned with the RSM to his office. Once we got to reviewing the subject of the meeting, I asked him why he was so concerned about my fitness. He replied he was not, he was more focussed on his own, that is why he wanted me to undertake the duty of ROS (Regimental Orderly Sergeant) for the duration of the Camp. This would entail me being more or less his gofer. This he freely admitted, at the risk of receiving a somewhat hostile response from me, "for I am well aware of your personality and quite often quick temper, so if you intend to have a rant let's get it over with now and remove that expression on your face".

He paused then said "well!" I replied, "I never knew you were such a Pussy Cat". He responded in words that indicated his wish that I vacate the office, his words as I left sounded like don't you dare say a word.

So it looked as though I would spend the whole fortnight driving Tom about from place to place wondering how many times I will hear the words "put him in the book Sergeant Neil, any 252s will have to wait until we return to Newcastle". That should keep me occupied for at least another week.

Had I only known what lay ahead of me I am sure I would not be so flippant, but that story has of yet been known to but a few, therefore I will cut to the chase and begin.

Everything appeared to be rolling along nicely, both at home and work. It brings to my mind that very soon a beautiful little girl will be coming home, our little baby Fiona.

So now, having developed an air of I can handle this, I started the preparatory work for the forthcoming training camp. This time I spent more time carrying out TA work than civilian work. There were also several journeys to Catterick but these to me were always an enjoyable diversion, for I would invariably meet someone from the past.

During all of this, we were informed GHQ were sending a team to carry out a CIV inspection on vehicles and equipment. This would be carried out in ten days' time. I felt that our unit had little to worry about, as the vehicles were of a very high standard and as far as I could see the equipment was in prime condition and accounted for.

All I can add to this is 'bring it on'.

Meanwhile at home Betty is continuing to develop quite enormous proportions. This obviously set my alarm bells ringing. I said to Betty "are they sure there is only one? It looks like twins". She advised me that it was our little girl and if they had got it wrong, I better be prepared to depart at the double. But we could rest assured that the doctors know what they're doing.

At this particular time things both at work and home were fairly calm and settled. Or so I thought, but no. I was awoken in the early hours of the morning by Betty to tell me to get dressed for little Fiona was on her way. There was no time to spare, I got Betty and David into the Land-rover and headed off to the Green Maternity Hospital, dropping David at my mothers. Betty and I had agreed this would complete our little family and I would never have to this again.

I had to leave her to go to work, but assured Betty and the staff I would return as soon as possible. I went to the TA centre to inform the RSM and hopefully make some arrangements regarding some time off as and when Betty and baby were coming home. I must confess emotions, which were high, and concerns were hand in hand.

As it turned out my concerns were unfounded and unnecessary for at 8:55am my darling Betty gave birth to a beautiful baby girl. I wanted the world to know that Fiona had arrived, mother and daughter were doing very well.

I was immediately ordered by my friend and comrade RSM Tom, to leave my work to him and go to visit my beautiful wife and daughter. I don't think I have ever felt so extremely happy and proud, at last our little family is complete.

It then suddenly dawned on me to visit my mother's home. I needed to break the news and see my little boy to let him know he now has a sister to play with and when they grow up, he can protect her. Then I thought I must sort myself out, for I had to focus on matters in hand. As things were, if I sat down for a cup of tea, my mind would begin to wander to the future. Trips to the seaside, or in the country and then the thrill of Christmas and the expressions on the children's faces when they see the city Christmas lights and the joy as they look at the big store windows. I am sure that time of the year is by far the most magical for young and old alike. Therefore, it was a case of put your cares on hold, put a smile on your face and hope good fortune will come your way.

The preparations for the new arrival were in place before Betty was taken into hospital. We also had a very good friend next door who had everything ready for our return with baby Fiona. Needless to say, David was besotted with his baby sister and kept going to look into the cot. I cannot recall any period that in any way would compare with this moment in my life. My joy, contentment and love were way off the scale. Boy, girl, home, car and all topped off with, to me, the most beautiful girl in the world, my dearest Betty. It was almost like a beautiful dream.

It was at this time I was offered a three-bedroom semi-detached house with garage and gardens front and rear, in my hometown Wallsend. I had a chat with Betty and we both agreed it was too good an opportunity to turn down.

So, an easy decision made as we knew the people vacating the property and it was in very good condition. Therefore, it was only a question of transport and for that I would try and call in an old promise made when I had to leave my former employer. Needless to say, my old colleagues, the "wild bunch", arrived the following Saturday with a pantechnicon (job done).

I am sure it must have been some sort of record for moving to a new house. The couple had left the almost new carpeting for us as they put it, to leave the house habitable until we can find time to choose our own carpets. So, my old workmates installed all the furniture under Betty's supervision. I must add, living up to their reputation, there was much laughter as they responded to her instructions with tugging of forelocks, bowing with yes ma'am thank you ma'am. Eventually the work and merriment drew to a close. I offered my old pals some remuneration for their efforts the respond was (I thank God) out of earshot of the more sensitive ears. "Off" was quite prevalent in the response. They reacted in an almost offensive attitude such as, "stick your money", "we thought you were our friend", so all I could say was "thank you!" As I wrote earlier of the time that I first became involved with this illustrious group of gentlemen (knights of the road), one-word springs to mind and that is, Unique! May Angels watch over them.

Their help and generosity appeared to be boundless as was their humour and resilience - outstanding.

When our working guests had taken their leave, the kiddies were tucked up and asleep giving Betty and I some free time to plan the next stage of our lives. It was that night I thought "I don't think it can get any better than this". The following morning, after giving as much help as I could, it was time to go to work at the TA centre. I went to my office and found a considerable quantity of mail to be dealt with, so I set to work to sort and distribute.

I had just about completed this when the RSM came into my office. We exchanged customary niceties and he inquired as to how Betty and the children were and had I been able to complete the move into our new house. I assured him yes without a hitch, even to the location of the furnishings within the respective rooms under Bettys supervision. My recollections of this were a lot of noise, my lady issuing orders, closely followed by threats of a reprimand should there be any form of retaliation or worse, if the poor unfortunate did not react with enthusiasm. And so, it all went off with lots of laughter. This memory will never leave me, my wonderful work mates and my beautiful witty wife.

Once more, time to move on. I felt that we had achieved so much in that past year. Our little family that we longed for, a very nice house in a desirable location and it seemed that I was almost back to full fitness. At last we had stability in our life.

Betty and I at home dressed for VJ Dance

Betty, lovely lady in uniform

Me on jungle patrol

Me and the band of brothers

CHAPTER 9

Camp

It was time to knuckle down and start work on planning for the annual training camp. On one occasion the RSM remarked how well I looked, I replied "it must have something to do with parenthood". His response was that it never affected him that way. Oh dear! I reflected that I must have got it wrong last time, "You're not a pussy cat you're a tiger", to which I was advised that "If you want to keep those stripes, you had better stop taking the p….". "I could ask Betty to have a word with Helen", that's Toms wife. She and Betty were both in the ATS. I think I liked him as a pussy cat. This said, he knows that there is no way I would behave like that if there was anyone else about. Before he left the office, he said not to hurry in the following morning if Betty needed a hand, adding 10.30 hrs would be soon enough. He would give me a call if something unexpected should turn up. I must confess we made a good team, and long I wished it to last.

As always, time marches on and in no time at all we were beginning to prepare stores and pack equipment for the annual camp, when everything accelerates. But having said that, it was nonetheless always orderly and efficient, under the watchful eyes of the QM and RSM. The layman would have no idea of the amount of planning effort that goes into such an exercise. And this is before we leave the TA centre.

LAST MAN STANDING

While writing this episode, it has just occurred to me that we are currently in the grip of a pandemic that requires a national screening scheme to track, trace and isolate to prevent the spread of the virus. Being such a mammoth task, who is called in at short notice? The Territorial Personnel of all three services, as so often happens in these cases. Always on hand, unsung heroes.

The reason for my digression will be fully explained at the end of the book.

Meanwhile the annual camp preparations were almost complete, and it would soon be time to move out. Let's hope we have good weather and a successful result on the Brigade Exercise.

I will now move on to my arrangements with Betty and the children who were to receive assistance from the district nurse, as well as from her friend from work who was to stay with her. I therefore knew she would be alright while I was away, and I hoped it would go over quickly. On the day before we were to depart Tom the RSM came to ask if it would be alright for his wife Helen to visit Betty. I assured him that she would be delighted to which he said, "they can talk about their former conquests when stationed at Colchester". I however doubted whether they were ever that way inclined.

So, to war, or something like it. Each squadron was given a designated route, so as not to create traffic problems on minor roads by keeping their distance. I would always instil into the driver, to be polite and respectful to other road users, emphasising to constantly keep in mind that you represent the British Army.

Then the RSM gave the order, Prepare to Move.

As far as I can recall, the move seemed to be accomplished without incident and with the individual squadrons arriving more or less on time. It did not take long for the installing of the personnel in their respective accommodation and once this had been accomplished it was time for the evening meal.

Then at 18.00hrs it was guard mounting. There was one guard which was divided into two guards, as in number 1 guard on the main camp, number 2 guard on the vehicle park. Of the two, the vehicle park was the most vulnerable and comprised of two sentries, one on the entrance the second would be the prowler. This would be the most important as it is situated on the A66 road. It is open and there had been several attempts to steal fuel and on one occasion a land rover. Therefore, it always necessitated a high standard of alertness and observation. The guard for the main camp comprised two sentries, one on the gate and a prowler.

So, in-camp life began. The first night's guard was arranged on arrival, but subsequent nights there will be a regulation guard mounting as the per book, with officers of the day and ROS (Regimental Orderly Sergeant). Everyone must read orders of the day on the squadron noticeboard to see if they are required for duty.

The first full day in camp began with myself as ROS, holding staff parade at the guard room, being present at the handover of the guard to the Regimental Police, meeting the new officer of the day and the RSM, and visiting the dining hall in company with the Orderly Officer and RSM. Shortly after this I received a message to report to the squadron leader's office. When I arrived there, also present were the 2IC and the RSM. The SL invited me to sit and began to advise me that he was having a leadership problem which the RSM and I could help to resolve. He then went on to tell me that he had been let down, there being one officer short of full strength which leaves 1st troop without a leader. If you and the RSM would like to discuss the matter, we will leave you here and Cpt G and I will have a tour of the camp. So off they went leaving Tom and I to sort things out, but he began by informing the SL that he was uncomfortable about the extent of my injury and was unconvinced with my fitness. As we were alone, I told him I was in good health and prepared for a new challenge to test myself. Tom's response was, "go for it Dave, just let them see what a 4th Hussar can do". So, mind made up and with Tom's approval, when the SL returned, we informed him of my decision. He said he was well pleased and would render me every assistance possible. I thanked him for his generous offer, but I hoped he would let me do it my way. His response was an affirmative to my suggestion, so I would now have to go and introduce myself to my troop. I contacted Sgt Stan who was the troop sergeant and as it happens, we were both in the same class at school. He did his national service in the Royal Navy but on release he enrolled in the TA. He rounded up the rest of the troop and when they were all assembled, I had two corporals, one lance corporal, ten troopers. On the equipment side, one Ferret Scout car, one land rover and one 15cwt truck.

As it happens most of them knew me as I had been their drill instructor when they joined up. Corporal G was a former Coldstream Guard, Corporal B was a TAVR, L/Cpl B also a TAVR. The troopers had little or no previous military experience. In reality, most of them had no grasp on the necessity or even the need for discipline. It was therefore imperative to bring this group to heel and this must happen in hours rather than days. I and Sgt Stan called all the troop NCO's and the three drivers to a meeting in my bunk. The last three I included as they had a sense of loyalty and responsibility and I had a gut feeling it might work. When they were all assembled, I informed them of my position and the reason for the meeting, which was to advise them that I was hoping they would be willing to assist me knock this shower into some sort of shape in the limited time at my disposal. I know I was gambling with my own reputation by expecting them to run the risk of alienating old friendships with someone they hardly know. But my feelings said, "what the hell, go for it". This I did and received the full backing of the NCO's and the drivers. With this support we had a hastily arranged meeting to acquaint my team of an outline plan for the next two days. On the following day the regiment will be holding a briefing prior to the Brigade Exercise. This left one day to get this troop into some semblance of order of preparedness. I told Sgt Stan and Cpl G to march the troop to the tank park and drill them until they sweat. "I will join you shortly, I just want to have a word with the RSM" and followed that with a wink. I was well pleased to see Sgt Stan had set them off at the double with Cpl G out front to set the pace and I haven't even started yet (I think back to those instructors at the JWS in Johor). I went to the orderly office to see the RSM and expressed my concern about the number of barrack room lawyers in this troop. So now that they have become my responsibility, I requested some time to get them sorted out as I was yet to be briefed on our role in the forthcoming Brigade Exercise. I advised him that the would-be awkward squad were down on the tank park at this time, being in the process of receiving a beasting from Sgt Stan and Cpl G, a former Coldstream Guard Corps of Drums and 17/21 Lancer. "I would be most grateful if you could spare me some time to go down there and reinforce my NCO's". He asked me to give him ten minutes, then follow him and stand on the side of the square until he indicated for me to join him. "I think these young fools don't know who they are dealing with". He told them how I had spent almost four years of my service with the Far East Land Forces in the steamy jungles of Malaya, most of the time involved in mortal combat against an elusive and deadly enemy. "So, I am giving you fair warning, don't try and mess about as he may wear three stripes, but he is now your troop leader. He and I have been associated for many years. Play the game and

133

you will be all the better for the experience of his knowledge and leadership. But beware of non-co-operation, for if you cross swords with him you will most likely lose, work with him and you will learn the value of true loyalty and comradeship and be a better man for it".

I must confess I was speechless as I stood there while Tom delivered his oratory to those would be potential failures. They were obviously uncomfortable, shuffling their feet and looking down and avoiding eye contact as the troop sergeant and corporal were quietly moving among their ranks, telling them to lift their heads or stop fidgeting.

This most unexpected, but much appreciated even in a way embarrassing, moment is and will remain indelibly etched on my heart, bless you Tom (Cometh the hour, Cometh the man). The remarkable thing was it had really hit the target for attitudes began to change, you could sense it and it was noticeable not only with the troopers but also the NCO's. They were much more aware of their rank and began to carry out their duties with much more panache.

We now had one more day to prepare for the Brigade Exercise. After breakfast, Sgt Stan and I attended a squadron O group and were briefed on the role my troop was to play. In short, we were to reconnoitre the enemy's right flank without being discovered, reporting to HQ any troop movements and gather as much information as possible. We and the other troops moved off from our dispersal point to begin our assignment. This required a good deal of careful movement and making use of any available cover that comes into our vision. Working from the scant information given at the briefing, we parked the troops vehicles in a grove of trees. I asked Sgt Stan to take a trooper to a rise in the land on the other side of the grove I had identified. That should give them some cover. "Let me know if it looks clear down to the road in the valley, or if there is any sign or movement of the enemy". It didn't take long before the trooper returned, more than a little out of breath. He advised me that the troop sergeant had sent him back to ask that I come and join him, keeping out of sight, Trooper P will guide me to where he was in position and watching. When I arrived, he told me what I had already seen. It was an enemy ferret scout car about 100yds away, the engine was running. The driver was in his seat and the commander was standing up in the turret talking on his radio with his back to us. At that point we were all concealed behind a dry-stone wall so the plan was that we would have to crawl about 50yds on hands and knees. Then, when I say go, we will be in position and we will quickly jump the wall. Trooper P held his gun on the driver while I and Sgt Stan disabled the radio. Then we won the star prize, their map board complete with its china-graph cover which was clearly marked to indicate and reveal the disposition of the opposition forces, plus their radio call signs and location of their headquarters. Shall we say game over, but that was just the first round.

The second round begins in three days' time and Tom has offered to give me a lift home in his land rover to see Betty and the children. An unexpected but most welcome interlude, but both Tom and I were back in camp in time for reveille. The next morning, I told Tom that I would join him for breakfast in the mess, as I wanted to check on my troop. I had a brisk walk down to their billet, on the way I met Stan coming toward me. I thought *"my God, what the hell have they been up to?"* "Hi Dave, glad to see you back". My response I think was along the line "I don't think I want to know". I then had to steel myself for something I had no idea what to expect. I entered their barrack room with a totally false portrayal of self-confidence, but fully prepared to blow my stack. As I made my entrance I stopped and looked the length of the room. Stan was in front of me and brought the room to attention. The room had already been thoroughly cleaned, beds were made up, the troop all appropriately attired in the dress of the day and it was only 07.15hrs. And they are all waiting to go for breakfast. I thanked all the NCO's and told all the members of the troop that I would have an in-depth discussion after 08.00hrs parade. I had decided to do this after a brief talk with Stan. This I would call a clear the air meeting and it will include a question and answer period which would be a two-way event and cover the subjects of discipline and loyalty.

So off we all went for breakfast. Stan and I to the Sergeant's Mess, where we had our meal with the RSM. He was delighted with Stan's handling of the situation and we would review the episode at the end of the camp. I myself thanked all the troop NCO's. Now we must think ahead to train and plan for phase two of the exercise, which would involve penetrating or, if you wish, infiltration. I prefer to use the latter term. Reason – it is challenging and if you approach the task with patience for real action, and if you are successful, you will not have been drawn into a firefight risking casualties or blowing the whole operation. The most effective elements in such an operation are stealth, silence and patience. "Therefore, this next phase, which will commence tomorrow morning, will give you all an opportunity to hopefully learn and assimilate. I think it only fair to ask you to follow the guidance you are receiving in your training. I tell you this for today your role is considerably changed from the original role. Due to cutbacks in the army, it is becoming more prevalent to mobilise members of TAVR, often to fill gaps in active front line combat units and this is why it is for your benefit to absorb as much knowledge as possible".

I don't think to continue the previous methodology was going to serve any further use or purpose. It would now appear that what previously had a potential to become a breeding ground for indiscipline, had now been completely turned about and we were well on the road to achieving some notoriety. Who can tell, on the last day of camp are we in line for an award? This was a possibility, providing that we could repeat our Phase One performance. With this in mind, I paused to look back at those first two days at Warcop and the amazing transformation that had taken place by two men who I knew from different phases of my life. First there was Tom the RSM who was my troop sergeant when I joined the 4th Hussars, and Stan the troop sergeant who was in the same class at school. It was they who were behind two truly outstanding pieces of oratory, delivered to a group of would be disobedient rabble who obviously had decided to be disruptive. It was abundantly clear that they had only enlisted to receive payment for their service. On the realisation of the army's requirements in their minds, their thinking being to be disobedient and so be chased home. Now however, they knew different and it appeared that they were learning to enjoy some of the challenges and hopefully beginning to take some pride in themselves, thanks to my colleagues.

Here we go into week two and dare I say the possibility of more accolades for the troop as we undertake our part in the second phase of the Brigade Exercise. For this part we would be moving to a more westerly area of the training ground. Our allotted position was facing south with a clear line of vision covering the north side of Shap Fell, our position on the right flank. I deliberately told some of my chaps to wander about and look as though they were preparing an observation post. As it was, the ground behind our position fell away quite sharply. When I considered the lads had given an impression of creating some sort of defensive position, I told them to act and gesticulate signs of annoyance. When I gave the order to stop working they were in the wrong location, they were all aware of what we were doing and after this unrehearsed display of bad acting staged for the entertainment of the opposition in the hope of misleading or confusing our opposition, we received a visit from the SL shortly before stand too. I gave him an outline of my plan to ambush at least one of their patrols at the same time explaining the deception act earlier that evening. He had a laugh and went on his way.

At last light everyone went to their designated position quietly. When in position, myself in one and the Sgt Stan in the other. Then slightly to the rear of us, I had placed the two corporals hoping that the enemy had taken the bait and would try to slip through what they now consider to be an abandoned position. Should they attempt to do that, I think it would verify that you don't mess about with Geordie corporals.

Well, the night progressed, time was slipping away, and I began to think that I had got it wrong. Then just before midnight all hell broke loose. The sky was illuminated by Vari-lites and the opposition walked into our trap. Our corporals had apprehended a sergeant and two troopers, and the umpire declared it a well-executed counterattack by the defence with prisoners captured. The exercise had been a success.

Now it was back to camp and begin preparing to return to Newcastle in the next few days. I was very proud of the troop, from all the outstanding NCO's to the rapidly developed small fighting unit that I can say it has been a joy and pleasure to command. But, as often happens, just as you think all is going well you discover *"no, it's damn well not"*. Sgt Stan informed me that trooper X has lost or misplaced a pair of army binoculars. Stan had trooper X with him and the lad was quite distraught as you may well imagine. I asked him could he recall when he last had them, he was sure it was in the forward OP on the night of the attack. I asked Stan to get one of the corporals to bring one of the land-rovers, it was Cpl G, so off we went. We had reached the location where the OP was, we both searched the post and surrounding area, all to no avail. We returned to the vehicle to go back to camp. Then this is the point where things began to kick off. I was very tired, not having any sleep for a long while and it would seem I fell asleep. The Corporal was driving, so I thought no worries. The next thing I remember was someone shaking me awake. It was a nurse who informed me that I had been in a traffic accident. My first reaction was to ask how my Corporal was. She said the army had taken him away. I then asked if he was alive? "I only know that the army took him away". I again asked if he was alive and eventually was advised that he was. They asked why I was so concerned. I told her that he had borrowed a cigarette off me. Soon it was explained to me that I had passed out for a while. I could see the screens around were closed. It was so quiet, and the nurses just glided in and out of my bed area. I think I began to lapse into what I could only define as short periods when I began a feeling of comfort and relaxation, as though I was in some form of transit. It would seem to me I must be dying but I am sure I would resist such thoughts. I think it must have been then that I heard voices and realised there were nurses and a man, who turned out to be surgeon, who had just finished working on me in the operating theatre. He told me that he would come to see me later. "Just try and rest and then we'll get your concerns sorted out after you have had a rest". I am not too sure, but I think that they had given me some form of sedative to make me sleep. It was trying to do its job, but my mind was fighting against it. I wanted to know if my wife had been informed and why had nobody come to see me. Eventually the sedative won, and I slept. When I woke there was the ward sister telling me that I had a visitor and so I did, it was the CO Lord R. He asked me what I regard as the mandatory hospital visitor questions and said that arrangements had been made for my wife to visit as often as she wishes, and she should be here any time soon. That was what I wanted to hear. He and I talked for a while and he said the RSM had a chat with him and told him that initially when I took command of that troop there was a potential for trouble, but some words of wisdom from the RSM followed by sensible but controlled guidance from the troop sergeant and the corporals resulted in a proud dedicated team. It was then time for the CO to depart and then the arrival I was longing for. Here she was. A friend and his wife had brought her in their car. They had a short chat with me, then said that they were going into the city and would be back later. Once on our own she became a little emotional, in fact I confess to feeling a little that way myself. But when things settled down, she brought me up to date about the children. David was asking when I was coming home. I told her that at the moment I had no idea, but the consultant will see me tomorrow and I would phone her and let her know. I didn't tell her that my injuries were quite serious, and some could be permanent. I later learned my deception of Betty had been a total waste of time and effort, as she was informed before I was. So, it would appear among my injuries were a broken bone in my neck, broken jawbone, fractured skull and spinal injuries.

It may well begin to give the impression that I am accident prone. Well, the more observant will have noticed that except for the very first occurrence at the age of three, all others were brought on by other people. That would be my defence and hope it puts the idea that I may be clumsy or worse still, a bit of a dipstick, to an end.

So, hospital life went on and it was decided to carry out another operation on my right arm which had been broken and was trapping a nerve. Another morning without breakfast. I declared to all my fellow martyrs that I will confront the surgeon and demand a rebate to cover loss of nutrition. Being an all-male ward there was from time to time some rather raucous occasions and as is my nature I was not averse to taking part in some of the more static pranks. So here it goes. On the ward was a young nurse who we all referred to as Ringo. She was very dedicated to her profession and being pretty, not averse to a compliment or the occasional wolf whistle. On the occasion I now write of, while giving me a bed bath behind the screens I informed her I could not give her a kiss and she really shouldn't be in bed with me. Unfortunately this prank went off like a damp squib for at that very moment, unbeknown to both myself and poor Ringo, to elevate the now embarrassing situation to a higher level, the sister, who was known to hold deep religious convictions, ordered the removal of the curtains leaving me with egg on my face, but minus fig leaf for other areas. There were other incidents, but it would seem on most occasions the staff were one step ahead of me.

My wife's visits were covered expenses wise if travelling alone, but often friends would bring her and it allowed them to visit. After three weeks they said that if I could walk the length of the ward unaided, I could go home. "If I can walk the length of the ward without aid, hard to do, but watch me". I succeeded and it was a taxi to the station and the train home. On arrival I was totally exhausted but had to pull myself together to see the kids. Towards the end of that not too long journey, I was beginning to develop a loss of confidence and a feeling of exhaustion and was fearful I would collapse when getting out of the taxi. But Betty came to the rescue with of all things a small bottle of smelling salts that managed to sustain me.

My parents were there to meet me as they had taken care of David and Fiona to let Betty collect me from the hospital.

David was quite excited and would keep climbing on my knee. It was so good to know I was home and I would cherish every moment of being once more reunited with my family and hopefully having time and guidance to achieve something as acceptable as possible to a healthy recovery. For I know I would not now be capable of fulfilling the physical requirements that would enable me to undertake any work in my previous employment as a soldier, or a trucker. I was aware that I would have my army pension to provide me some foundation to build from. That at least gave me some confidence to work on. Then it was time to debate the subject with Betty to see what we can come up with.

As it happens, I had an old friend who was a bricklayer who built or rebuilt garden walls in his spare time and he invited me to join him on this venture. I accepted and found it most rewarding and it could be enjoyable working out in the fresh air.

At this particular moment in time, the MOD doctors declared me unfit for further military service (quotation from an old sweat *"the day will dawn, the lord will say you've done your time, so file away")* and here endeth another lesson.

My first reaction was one of relief, followed by a mountain of grief and sorrow for so many old comrades who did not return and those who did but couldn't cope and ended in institutions or worse. May the good lord comfort and cherish them. While on this subject, I hope at the end of this book to throw a little light on a soldier's opinion of the pathetic handling of their plight. Or to be more precise, on behalf of the Queen who is always portrayed by politicians as the head of the armed forces and when we enlist, we swear an oath of loyalty towards. I will not pursue this subject any further at this moment.

I will now return to my chronicles and at this point emotions are very prominent, as I sit here trying to recall events which took place all those years ago. I feel such great sadness that my now long-lost comrades have been deprived of all those years and opportunities. Sleep well bonny lads.

So, moving on with my life. It was a series of medical interviews and assessments, then much to my surprise the panel's decision was – unfit to fulfil medical requirements. That was it, no expression of "regret to inform you…. etc". I was not looking for or expecting any form of accolade, but a thank you for your loyalty and service would have been nice. Probably not in the makeup of those Whitehall warriors, perhaps eager to vacate this almost hostile place and its somewhat primitive people. Thank God that is not the way the regiment dealt with my departure, for those officers were not only gentlemen they were Geordie Gentlemen. The RSM organised a farewell party in the Sergeant's Mess and invited the Colonel and his wife, also some of the other officers and wives. For this to happen illustrates the true spirit of comradeship. This above all other things, is what I will always miss.

This glorious event was arranged and orchestrated by the RSM and need I say, there was no lack of attention to detail. A most wonderful occasion at which I was presented with an engraved Stirrup Clock by the Commanding Officer and for Betty a beautiful bouquet. Well, after a wonderful evening with friends and former comrades, I was well pleased with the very generous and complimentary words that were spoken on this not to be forgotten event.

And so, to bed. Next day, Betty and I would embark on creating yet another new life for ourselves, and that spirit of adventure was still alive. Nothing would daunt us, with a love so strong and our little family, we could and would always meet every challenge.

Therefore, with the dawn we would begin to work out our approach to this new venture. I felt that we needed to approach this matter with a degree of caution, in other words, avoid any risk of possible accident black spots that could result in me having to visit yet another hospital. There was no rush as we were financially sound. My new employer was an odd-job man and would appreciate some assistance. He assured me that there was nothing that I would find at all detrimental to my health and well-being, for he was well aware of my physical limitations. Let's say it was basically fetch and carry. Therefore, bring it on.

CHAPTER 10

Dance the Night Away

It was obvious this little job would never be enough to sustain us, so I would have to develop something else to subsidise my income. It was then that Betty came up with the idea to run a dance in our local club. She was an excellent dancer and had the ability to teach dancing which was our favourite pastime. I suppose being as both our parents also went dancing, you could say it was in the blood.

The opportunity came our way because of things we were unaware of. The chap who ran the dance at our local club had a falling out with the committee and walked out leaving them with no cover for the following Sunday night. One of the committee members knew Betty and I were regulars at that Sunday event and so he advised her that it was cancelled. She immediately said, "no problem, Dave and I will give it a try". When she informed me of this, I suppose I just quietly went into a blind panic, for we had no equipment and neither had the club. I had to think what to do. The idea of doing the dance was a golden opportunity to break into the dance business, which can be quite lucrative if you can become established. So, I called at the club and received an assurance we would be reimbursed. With that matter resolved, we could make a mad dash to purchase the necessary equipment. This left us with sufficient time to install the gear at the club, work out a programme of dances and select the appropriate music. If I had enough time, then I could brush up on my DJ patter.

As it happened, Betty and I had a good selection of records for dancing to, both sequence and ballroom and a little bit of jive or rock and roll too. So, there you go (hit the floor the great days are back). The club were good to their word and we were promptly and suitably reimbursed. As the room was not in regular use until the dance on Sunday, we had programmed the first night and had the opportunity to rehearse once or twice during the week while the club was closed. I must confess to being rather apprehensive, but my beloved was the epitome of *"like cool man!"* How does she do it? No doubt she was so very special not just to me but to everyone.

At last it was show time at the Westholme Farm Ballroom, to the Sound of *Switched On Swing.* Dancing to the classic favourites of bygone days, no cover charge and bingo in the 20-minute interval.

So much for my flamboyant approach to what my mind had as a taste of "stardom". That would be until about 45 minutes before the first dance, when with as much dignity as one could muster, I froze in what was sheer blind panic. My first thought *"this is sure to undermine Betty's confidence"*. Like hell it did! She told me to sit down have a drink, then say to yourself you're not a star and most of the people here, I know. I said "what if I make a right twit of myself?" Her reply came straight back at me,

LAST MAN STANDING

"if that's what they came for, then they can go home happy. Present yourself as you did when we practised the other day, just be in control or look that way".

Needless to say, following as it would appear a direct order, I took to the stage introduced Betty and followed with a brief explanation as to how we are taking over the Sunday night dance at the invitation of the club committee. I then thanked everyone there for their support.

Launching the dance with a quickstep to the music of the Ray Conniff Orchestra called *Swonderful,* a very impressive and swinging foot tapper, the evening was underway. I was both pleased and relieved that most of those attending showed their appreciation at the end of the evening. I would not attempt to delude myself or others that it was a massive success, I noticed over the following weeks the people who appeared to be dissatisfied or downright anti and these just seemed to fade away. However, much to our delight they were quickly replaced by new dancers. And so, we carried on as the numbers attending began to increase, to a point when Betty suggested we give some thought to starting a dance club. This would be a Thursday evening session to help those who would like to learn the dances, from Betty and a dear friend teaching or coaching. I had a meeting with the Chairman, and he gave it the nod. So, we commenced on a non-profit making members club run by a committee of 4. Once more it was a great success and always well attended.

Betty in high spirits, New Year's Eve dance

Me playing the Dj

Me with some of my brother, night out, Taiping

The idea of the mid-week dance club quickly took off. It seemed that Betty had given our clientele the feeling that they and we were as one, working together to make the project a success. This felt to us somewhat more than a little achievement. Those were halcyon days, or should I say nights. They will live in my heart and mind forever. It would also be appropriate to mention that there was a spin-off from this Thursday night venture, in that it resulted in an increase in the numbers attending the Sunday night dance.

I was always an early riser, so would make myself a cup of tea. Betty was certainly not an early riser. This left me to watch the news and enjoy my cuppa. Now and then I would prepare a family breakfast and for some strange reason always ended up washing the dishes. But I didn't mind for I was so happy and contented. My life was almost like a dream for I thought I had all that I could wish for. Two now rather grown kids and to me the most beautiful and talented girl in the world. Then add to all that what I would call as possibly the most rewarding form of employment one could wish for my love of music dancing and meeting people. Life had settled into a comfortable pattern. I had so much more time at home compared to earlier years and jobs. The kids were now at a stage of being able to look after themselves to a fairly large degree.

It was nevertheless during this phase in my life, after an unusually disturbed night's sleep I got out of bed made a cup of tea and found myself thinking that something was wrong.

LAST MAN STANDING

We just don't go through life having so much good fortune. My life has never been that way. Shortly after, Betty came down got herself a cup of tea and sat with me. Then with more than a trace of annoyance in her voice, she asked what was bothering me. I told her about my concern. She then laughed and said, "Well lucky you, I have that feeling almost every day and have done so for quite some time. Just forget it and move on". I had a feeling this was not intended as a word of advice but more of an order. Therefore, I thought she should not speak to me in that way, then followed her instruction. That will teach her a lesson, who does she think she is, head of the household? Good lord, I think she knows for I certainly do.

Life had settled into a fairly routine pattern. Monday choose dances and music for the Thursday dance club. Tuesday the same for the Sunday night dance. Betty housework me clean car or work in garden. In between those times shopping or what we called leisure time, which covered a multitude of opportunities such as swimming, snooker, visiting, or perhaps just chilling out.

I think it was just about this time I was out walking and as there was a convenient bench, I sat down and it being so quite I began to think of how far we had come since we first met. I began to think about the time I met Betty and how quickly we realised we had fallen in love and how that love had endured for almost four years when we were half a world apart. It never faltered. If it were possible,

DAVID NEIL

I think it grew stronger. Things had become so full of joy and at last tranquillity appeared to have arrived and any form of turbulence was banished. All that we required was time to support and enjoy our family, our home and hopefully good health too.

I am prompted to digress slightly for a moment and reflect. By now David had settled into a career. From an early age he had developed an interest in trains. In his younger years, whenever I'd had the opportunity, we'd take walks up through the nearby farm where just beyond lay the East Coast Main Line. High speed express trains hauled by the world renowned Deltic locomotives would occasionally speed by. Who could keep a young boy away from that? As he grew older, he would take himself off to Newcastle Central station to meet friends, watch the trains and take the occasional train ride when he'd saved up enough to do so. I am sure those who know my family and particularly my son David, will know where this passion for trains took him. Not directly though. After leaving school his first offer of employment came in the form of a job at the Department of Health and Social Security (DHSS), which we advised him to accept. This he did, and it would be almost two years before the call from the railways came. He fulfilled his dream by joining British Rail at the age of 18, as a traction trainee, a role which in effect was a trainee train driver. From here he went on to qualify as a train driver before eventually moving on into management. A spin off from that, a very proud father.

LAST MAN STANDING

This came about quite strangely however, as the letter offering David the job at British Rail had actually got lost in the post. Betty received a phone call from the Personnel Manager at Newcastle Central Station enquiring if David was still interested in the job. "Oh yes!" was her reply. David was at work at the DHSS when she rang and broke the news to him. He needed to speak with his manager to see how quickly his notice period would be. David's boss knew how much trains meant to him and was able to fast-track his notice. The move went through with no problems and David was on the way to fulfilling his dream. But a word of praise is due to that personnel manager. He could easily have assumed that David was no longer interested, but instead made the effort just to check for sure. We are so grateful, thank you sir. So, not at all bad at such an early age for my boy. My pride was there for him from the day he was born, so as a very young man he had at that time achieved the goal he had aimed for. My boy always prepared to step in when required.

My darling Fiona was also doing very well and stayed on at school to do her A-levels. Betty was having driving lessons. It felt a bit like I had been side-lined. But when I asked Betty, how come everyone else is studying or preparing for some type of test? The explanation I received from my beloved, was that she had told the kids to leave me alone, as I had a lot on my mind helping to sort things out with the various projects I was involved with, such as the dances the club and now also the National Malaya & Borneo Veterans Association (but more about that in the next chapter). She said I also needed some rest and relaxation. To allay what may be possible concerns of the more inquisitive reader, my wife was in full support and well acquainted with my actions. Those who knew her well could confirm she was an extremely witty and bright lady who was my 24/7 supporter and adviser. I would never have undertaken to have taken on the role of Club Chairman, which I went on to do, without her.

CHAPTER 11

National Malaya & Borneo Veterans Association

It was not too long before a problem made its appearance. Now one may think, is this really a problem? It could be, and we had no desire for it to further develop. To elaborate, someone had enquired about hiring us to provide some music from the 1940's and 50's, at a dinner to celebrate a Golden Wedding. We naturally would have to discuss this approach. As we had never undertaken this class of event before, it was wise to review what may be involved at such a function. It would have been more manageable and acceptable if we knew who we were dealing with and so we decided to tell them that we were fully booked and offered our apologies.

As a result of this, we decided we would only consider ex-service association functions in future. This decision was influenced by the fact that I had just learned of the formation of an association for Malayan Veterans and had sent off an application for membership. I was as you might well imagine, quite a little more than interested, though I felt that it had been rather late in its creation. I lost no time in passing on the news to my brothers of those now long-gone days and I had a dream in my mind of someday returning with Betty for a holiday, now that hostilities were long been and gone.

Shortly after sending off my application, I was contacted by several other veterans who lived in the local area and who had served in both campaigns (Malaya and Borneo) – their common bond. They comprised of representatives of all three services. It was shortly after this that we all received notification of the first AGM. I and two other members attended with our wives.

There is not a great deal I can say about the meeting, other than it appeared very confusing and at times out of control with two or three groups jockeying for power. However, by the end of the meeting, there was a National Executive Committee (NEC) formed and our little party returned home to plan forming a branch on Tyneside. This task was undertaken by what I would call the Founding Fathers of this branch. We advertised in the local press and regional TV for new or existing members to attend a meeting, for the purpose of recruiting new members and electing branch officers and a committee. This would take place at the Westholme Farm Social Club, Wallsend.

The meeting took place and it was gratifying to see such a good turnout. It was decided that the branch would be known as the Tyneside Branch of the National Malaya & Borneo Veterans Association. Then it was time to nominate the committee. I found myself being nominated to the position of branch chairman; John Sweeney filled the post of secretary and Tom Nisbet would take on the role of Treasurer, these being the officers needed to start business.

LAST MAN STANDING

The first thing we had to address was the question of finance to help administer the branch effectively and to purchase a small amount of office equipment and stationery. I well recall our extremely efficient new secretary negotiated a lottery grant which covered the purchase of a computer and branch standard. This was so typical of John, any task he was given no matter how difficult he was an enormous asset to the setting up and development of the branch. Sad to say he is no longer with us. God Bless.

The branch grew quite quickly in those early days. It was strong and loyal. There appeared to be more than a little dissatisfaction in some of the branches in other areas of the country, but here in the north-east we were determined to keep this dream alive. So, we embarked on canvassing all the branches to support us in keeping the association together and work to progress it forward by strengthening the bond between branches. After a while we began to receive a substantial number of supportive replies. It was amazing the number involved in this very quiet revolution. Out of I think 23 branches if my memory serves me correctly, only 3 did not respond. Therefore, at our next branch meeting John informed the branch members that he would be nominating me to stand for the office of National Chairman at the next AGM. Much to my amazement this appeared to be unanimously supported. I could only thank them all and said I hoped I would not let them down.

I suppose I could say that this was a transition into another phase of my life, with the emergence of the NMBVA and the prospect of perhaps becoming the National Chairman in the not too distant future. To be honest I was not too sure if I was really all that keen to take on such a heavy mantle. I was wishing it to be easier for me to say, *"thanks but no thanks"*. But I must admit that I think the old sense of adventure won the day and this was being fuelled by feedback John was receiving from other quarters, that I would have a lot of support in the forthcoming election. So, it became a case of what the hell, let's go for it.

Meanwhile Betty and I had been approached by the president of the Burma Star Association to book us for their dance being held in the British Legion club in Gateshead, with an open invitation to any of our members to attend. Though it was not apparent at the time, it was the birth of a bond of comradeship between our two branches that survived until the demise of that association. Even at that point, their president and two members were integrated into our branch at their request, until there was only one left who sadly can no longer attend because of ill health. Bless 'em all.

I recall that at that particular period, we had several projects on the go, but not to the point where they would cause any disruption or problems. Though it could become challenging if or when I should take the position of National Chairman.

I desperately wanted the Malayan Veterans Association to succeed, for it was long overdue and to me it had be pursued to its full potential and not be permitted to fragment and fade. If we let that happen, we would have failed our comrades, those who we had to leave out there forever in our hearts.

Therefore, press on regardless was to become our watchword, for the thing of most importance was for the goal to be achieved, through honesty, dedication and above all loyalty. I must emphasise that this was the very early days of the branch, when those qualities were extremely prevalent. This was a great help in developing a strong bond. Unfortunately, and regrettably, as time went on an element became involved in the administration who I feel had no idea of the principles and objectives of such a body. As in the armed forces there is a chain of command, in this instance the committee. This was so sad, for what they wanted could have been achieved by going through the usual channels, causing some collateral damage only. The core of the branch remained loyal to the association and the branch committee and as quite often happens after a storm comes the sunshine. On this occasion that was in the form of a group of retired Gurkhas who more than made up for what I would call a shortfall in the branch membership. For me no loss but a mammoth gain.

One final point prompted by this subject. I have noticed on my ever-changing journey through life, the number of people who it seems try to make changes based purely on what's in their own mind. Because they go about it in a completely wrong way, they run the risk of alienating those they are trying to persuade. I regret to say I have seen this at all levels. It was never my intention to go down this road and I have one might say digressed, please excuse me. However, something happened very recently, which made me think about how some people perceive loyalty and dedication. I won't elaborate any further on the events I have in mind. Sadly though, it leaves me even at this stage of my life to ponder and question, are some people devoid of any sort of feelings? I class them as moral rejects.

Back to the NMBVA and time was getting ever closer to the AGM and the election, which had me more than a little concerned that if I was elected to office, I would be right in the front line. I was hoping that I could carry it off. My confidence was not at that point particularly high and one evening sitting with Betty in the lounge she asked, "was I worrying about the Chairman's job?" I admitted that it was a little. She told me not to worry about it disappointing her, if I should wish to take a step back and pull out. "Is that what you want me to do?" I asked, to which she replied "no!" In fact, it was quite the reverse, she thought I should go for it, "you've always enjoyed a challenge; you look to have a good team and seem to trust them". She then went on to inform me that should I appear to be losing my commitment, then she herself would give me a kick up the backside. She was fully convinced that I had the ability and qualities of leadership. I drew her attention to the fact that leaders were usually the first ones to be shot down, which I'd thought was a very good response. She suggested that it was not so much a response, more of a wish.

With those words of encouragement ringing loudly in my ears, it was time to depart for the AGM and the election. So off we went. The branch members and wives travelled by coach, but we went by car as we would only be there for one night and win or lose would travel home tomorrow. We all arrived about the same time, with a brief period of hand shaking and much to my amazement a substantial number from other branches came over to wish me luck in the forthcoming election. That was nice and a boost to my lagging confidence. My opponent was a very likeable gentleman who I shall refer to as J. His campaign agenda was to create strong bonds within the association and co-operation with other associations of a like mind. So at the meeting the following morning I stated if elected that I would work with the committee to put an end to any further infighting and squabbling, try to unite any opposing factions and in conclusion set up a transparent administration that would always be prepared to listen to branches and members concerns.

I was elected by a large majority and just to keep the record straight, my opponent became my vice chairman. We worked well together for many years through some extremely difficult times, with a potential to cause stressful side effects. But at that time, good fortune decreed that we had what I consider the very best executive committee for the situation at that time. I don't intend to elaborate any further on this subject, other than to make it clear that my last observations are in no way intended to be a criticism of any subsequent executive committee. If it appears that way to any of them, then I apologise unreservedly.

After the meeting concluded it was time for Betty and me to return home, as we had to go to work that evening to fulfil our commitment to the club in providing the dance music on the Sunday night. That was our bread and butter job and after that we could then hopefully enjoy a day of rest on the Monday. This was the thing we were wanting on our return home, a full day to chill out and with the assistance of good friends and family our wish was granted and very much appreciated.

Therefore, another step along the road to what I think of as my destiny. There may be those that think that remark was appropriate and some it may appear out of context, but I think you will understand as you progress towards the end of the book. I am motivated and driven by my sense of loss, which at times remains quite overwhelming, when trying to recall memories from by-gone days when love and joy were ever present, and one had the comfort and support of the one you love. If you allow those emotions to take you over, you may well drown in your own tears. Therefore, my only defence to thwart this destroying situation, is finding a true friend who has been through the mill and there like you and you then discover peace of mind. I did and it worked. I still live on my own. Presently I am in lockdown and deprived of having my two very caring friends to visit me.

LAST MAN STANDING

So, where were we? Ah, yes. I now needed to organise and prioritise my work time giving what was for the present first and what was pending, but I had two trustworthy friends to help. John the branch secretary who had volunteered to handle some of the Association work, which is essentially what he had been doing alongside me on shall I call it the election campaign. I can't speak too highly of him.

My other trustworthy friend, my darling Betty wife and mother of my children, who was more than capable of handling our commitment to the club if I was to be unavailable on association business. That would only happen if I was called upon for a matter which required some urgent attention, otherwise any problem would be dealt with at the next AGM.

Initially this arrangement was working, and we were making gradual progress, but to me it was never enough. I and the members of the NEC had a feeling of unease. Then after a while, things began to settle down and eventually we could recognise more enthusiasm among the membership. The association Patron attended our reunion for the very first time. He and I had a long in-depth discussion before dinner, after which I accompanied him around the dining room to introduce him to some of our members. We then had a photograph taken with all of the NEC and he was presented with a bottle of Whisky, after which he said to me very quietly when he took his seat "I thought it might be a bottle of Newcastle Brown Ale". I replied, "are you ready for that yet Sir?"

165

Sadly, he and I were never able to share our company again for Sir Nigel passed away shortly after. I had become aware that he was not too well. He had given me a list of prominent names to contact as potential successors, as he thought that would be some assistance in maintaining continuity if such change became necessary. He assured me they were all officers of the highest calibre and all had seen service in the Malayan Emergency, or the Borneo Conflict and he had advised them of my name and position within the association. As a footnote to this, when we heard of his demise Betty and I were told we would be most welcome to visit, which we did and spent some time with Lady Anna, her two daughters and baby.

Although several years have passed by since that sad time, I remain in touch with Lady Anna occasionally and much to our delight she honoured us all when she attended our re-dedication service at St Paul's Cathedral in 2017. A charming lady it has been my privilege to have the acquaintance of.

So back to my pursuit of a patron, and with a great deal of luck or good fortune I made contact with Sir Garry and made him aware of what was involved. I outlined some of the many good points and acquainted him of the not so good issues too. He informed me that Sir Nigel had already fully briefed him but had added that if I were to approach him, to let me present all of this in my own words. After my delivery, he told me that he would be most honoured and proud to be the head of such an admirable and worthy association, which

Me with Association President
Sir Garry Johnson CB, OBE, MC

Me with Gurkha comrades

Buckingham Palace garden party celebration

NMBVA Memorial Arboretum

embraces all the services from the Commonwealth Nepal and the UK. Thank goodness someone who has both knowledge and experience of the emergency and the confrontation. My wish now was to meet with him, which I was sure would arrive soon enough. So, stand easy and rest assured that day was to dawn.

The dances at the club were doing very well. We did get enquiries to take private bookings, but turned them down as they were mainly at the weekend and we were invariably busy with the dance on the Sunday, only leaving Saturday which we preferred to keep for ourselves to perhaps watch TV or a video and go to meet our friends at the club. There was always cheerful conversation and a game of bingo. The bonus, we could walk there and back from home when we'd had a drink. Just another little joy of life.

In writing this book I have deliberately avoided drifting off into what one could only call a recipe for boredom, by filling page after page of uninspiring and often repetitive ordinary mundane lives which would be of little or no interest. I am quite sure my decision to adopt this policy will meet with the approval of the reader. If I am incorrect in my decision, I will give you my assurance that my intentions were to try and dish up more meat than vegetables. If in doing this I have failed at my age (what the hell), I won't have time to try again.

Once more we were approached regarding a booking for a function, but this time it was a veteran's association and so we accepted.

On the night of this event, which was being held in another club not too far from our own, it turned out that club had a husband and wife team who were dance teachers. They were resident there and we were appearing on a night they were not working. It appeared that some of the veterans attended that clubs' dances. Betty and I had a feeling there was initially a trace of hostility or perhaps a nicer way of putting it, I think resentment. I am pleased to say it soon vanished once the dance got underway. During the interval some of the people who obviously were regular attendees at this clubs' dances approached Betty and I to say how much they were enjoying a different approach to the presentation and the music. This was very flattering but left us both just a little uncomfortable. You may ask, why would we be concerned? My answer to that is, "how would we feel if the shoe was on the other foot?" Threatened and uncomfortable. I live by the principal of do unto others as you would have them do unto you, therefore in our eyes as we were on, shall we say their territory, behave with dignity and don't attempt to take advantage of what may be a favourable situation. So, to conclude this episode, it was wonderful and in many ways rewarding, topped off with some prolonged applause at the end of the evening.

The following morning after breakfast Betty washed up and I dried after which we made the coffee and retired to the dining room for our coffee and discussion on the previous night's event and then we rechecked the Sunday night dance programme.

LAST MAN STANDING

On the following day it was time for my call to John who had agreed to deal with all association correspondence and emails. I offered to visit him at his home. This he thought was an excellent idea, for he had drawn up a list of branches and their secretaries who were fully committed to backing me and the new committee in our endeavours to advance and develop this promising but as yet not fulfilled fledgling of a long overdue association. Therefore, as you may well imagine there was much to be done. Having reached this point, I think it acted as an incentive to push on. I was, I must admit, more than a little frustrated by the amount of time which appeared to have been lost by leaving it too long before that AGM was called, to get the organisation installed and functioning. Then there was what we would refer to as the what's and why's questions that we were bombarded with, most of which we simply could not respond to for we were not in possession of the answers. All we could do was acknowledge receipt of their enquiry, which would be kept on file and reviewed periodically. That would be as and when the matter should come to light.

Whilst all this organising was taking place, one has to remember that I had a wife and family who I doted upon. So, there was no way that they would be pushed into the background come what may. Therefore, I always set time to talk with them.

Well as I have pointed out on several occasions, the reader will hopefully have realised once more the absence of what I regard as irrelevant information that I am sure would

171

be of little interest. Therefore I will carry on with the things I think may be more worthy of inclusion. As I am now wheelchair bound and thinking back to this period, what I am writing about quite frustrates me. I have always been a very active person with a sense of adventure who was not afraid to go the extra mile to achieve my goal.

Back in those now long-gone days, I would bend my knee to no man. But when I joined the army, I was taught to control my temper and walk away. It was only a very odd occasion I lost my cool for I must set a good example to my children.

So, reflecting on our basic routine, it was dance programming Monday night, dance club Thursday night, club dance on Sunday night. Then probably once a fortnight a trip into what I would prefer to think of as the most interesting city in the United Kingdom canny Newcastle upon Tyne and that is totally my biased opinion. I am entitled to let that be known as the book is being written on Tyneside therefore, I am claiming diplomatic immunity.

I must confess that at this moment in time, I am having great difficulty tracing exactly the various periods we are in. So I crave your indulgence, for I am quoting real life incidents involving real people. So I shall just press on till I come to a subject or some such happening which may arouse the readers interest and during this time I'm sure you will understand there would have been an unnecessary period of complete boredom and I am sure that is not what the reader would want.

In regard to the Malayan Veterans, work to clear the air and ensuring the correct information was forwarded to all of the branch secretaries was ongoing, as the new NEC got to work on the association books and trying to unravel the accounts. As far as I was involved, this was in communications and the invaluable assistance of our own branch secretary made this task much easier. We had to do most of this work at Johns house, for he had a computer and a lot of space for the storage of files and regalia.

At branch level we were beginning to receive some appropriate wall pictures and plaques of the regimental type. At the same time the Westholme Farm Club granted the branch use of the lounge rent free indefinitely, now that we had the blessing and support of the Club Committee, for which we were very grateful. As an anecdote, I was told about a stranger a first-time visitor to the club who was interested in the wall decorations. He enquired of the committee man who was selling the bingo tickets, "is this a British Legion club?" he was quickly told "no, but it is ex-service!"

Quite some time after that, I received a phone call from my old friend Dick at the Burma Star Association, to ask if Betty and I would like to provide some background music to a function in the Northumbria University Student Union Hall. It was to celebrate the anniversary of VJ Day and there would be a very large number of guests. When I asked Dick how many, his response knocked me sideways. He said, "I think about a thousand and they might be televising it as there is a very large party from Canada attending and possibly the Lord Mayor". I told him I would put Betty on the phone, as she was the one who dealt with the bookings. He muttered something about "chicken". I gave the phone to her, she listened and then said, "no problem Dick". I did have a little more sense than to say anything.

Following my dearest's rather cavalier response to this challenge and the knowledge that we only had two weeks to find out and assess the full and detailed requirements to organise such an enormous undertaking, her response was "the cheeky bugger, oh don't be such an old woman". My immediate reaction being, shut your mouth Dave you won't win. It was probably the expression on my face that prompted her next reaction when she said, "I'd better make you a cup of tea". Definition – She wishes to be my friend.

Now that I have put her in her place! It was time to carry out some research into the layout of the venue, it's accessibility and availability. The latter being to corroborate the details I had initially. Just as well I did, as I was told I would have to make an appointment to see the Hall Manager, who it turns out was available at that very moment if I wished to meet her. I took advantage of this bit of luck and met the lady. She asked me what my requirements were, and she gave me quite a shock by telling me that there was no need to bring anything other than the music. If I wished I could just MC the function and she would provide the DJ, a young chap who would put on whatever music I required. Ho ho, I could work any time under these conditions and in a perverse sort of way I almost did, but I digress.

Upon my return home I gave Betty the full details of the setup at the university and how I would only have to announce or act as Master of Ceremony. She asked if I thought I could handle that and I replied, "oh I think so, after all I do it at every dance we do". "But not in front of a thousand people and they don't all come from these parts", she pointed out. I just couldn't resist the urge to reply (in my Geordie twang), *"if thi divant na wot am sayin, thi shouldn be gannin"*. Unfortunately, as too often the case, my timing was way off the mark, as she was cleaning the window and I received a cold wet shammy leather on the back of my neck. I'd resolve this disgraceful incident; it was time to stamp my authority in my home. I told her that I would go and make the coffee darling. She immediately put her arms around me said that I was so domineering "the cream is in the fridge lover boy".

I called to see Dick and finalise the details for the reception at the university and gave him the general background music.

The day prior to the event Betty and I set to prepare a wide selection of music for the event. This was time consuming, but less than difficult. We now had a large range of quality

175

music that we were confident would facilitate most tastes at this type of occasion. As it was an afternoon function it could go on beyond its normal finishing time. This we normally wouldn't like to occur but on this occasion, we were accepting and prepared for it.

The next morning, I loaded up the music and our clothes into the car and left early to ensure everything we needed was in place. We met the technician who was in the process of assembling the record decks and sound equipment. We both found this chap very helpful his name was Stan and although none of us were aware, we were destined to get together at a later date. Having completed all the checks and found all was in order, Betty and I went to our dressing room to change into more formal attire and prepare for the arrival of the guests and the official party. On their arrival Dick had insisted that we were introduced, so that people were made aware of which association we belonged to, our presence was explained and the connection to the Burma Star Association.

I had asked my assistant (for the day) to play some unobtrusive easy listening music while the reception was in progress. I'd set the appropriate music to one side for that purpose. It appeared to go down well, so it would seem we were off to a flying start.

In the main most of the guests were mingling and it looked as though there was a lot of meeting old friends and making new ones. Meanwhile Betty was having conversations with some of the Burma Star wives. Then I notice one or two had got on the dance floor and were dancing, so I chose some dance records and gave them to Stan. I would tell him which ones to put on and if the floor begins to fill turn the volume up, but never too loud. Within two or three dances the floor was full.

I noticed a chap going over to Betty and he asked her to get up and have a dance with him. As the hostess she obliged. He then shortly after came over and asked if I would play a foxtrot. I told Stan and handed him a record with a very nice tune. I saw him go back across to ask Betty for this dance. In my mind I thought "oh oh, here we go", as we encounter at least one at every dance and have a plan to stop them. And she put this into action here. "Well you better ask my husband, that's him on the stage". I know the sign and when he looked up at me, I smiled and shook my head. Good grief I thought some people can't take a hint for he came over to me and said, "she said she was your wife, is that correct?" I replied. "I hope so, because she is the mother of my two children and the manager not a hostess. As for her referring you to me, I thought it was a clear indication it would not be approved of". Apparently, he went and complained to Dick who confirmed to him that what I had said was perfectly true, "It is their business and Betty is the manageress". He also added that Betty and I were very dear friends of his and suggested this chap be a little more cautious when asking a lady up to dance. I only refer to this small incident not for us, but for Dick who had been upset by it. We dealt with it very quickly and quietly, so the only potential blot was promptly eradicated. Reflecting on this, it was not an unusual occurrence with my dear wife being so well dressed and attractive there was always the possibility that some probably unaccompanied chap would take a chance and ask her for a dance. This situation was almost eradicated by Betty and her friend who would look out for the latter-day Fred Astaire's and the friend would as you say head them off at the pass. This was usually in our club and eventually the practice appeared to happen very rarely until it discontinued.

That little incident aside, the whole event was considered a huge success. There was much hand shaking and expressions of praise and appreciation, with lots of thank you's.

Moving on to our next challenge whatever that would be, the work we had just completed left us exhilarated, with a feeling of fulfilment and satisfaction. We were very satisfied, in that we felt that our involvement and performance had been as proficient and professional as could be achieved.

Nice though it might be, we could not waste time basking in our success. There are other commitments to be addressed and therefore I couldn't afford to sit and ponder. There were my commitments to the members of the Association and above all my devotion to my wife and family. To quote the Bard "this above all; to thine own self be true". Please excuse me for that small digression. I could not get in touch with Will to get his permission, but I have a very strong feeling I will be able to ask him shortly.

LAST MAN STANDING

Returning to the time we were asked by a very special friend to arrange an important event for the Burma Star Association at the Students Union Hall of Northumbria University, I mentioned we would meet up again with Stan. Well, we were back together once more. Apparently, this new booking was to co-ordinate and present a once a month a programme of modern ballroom and sequence dancing. The times would be varied with tea dances at 1:00pm and dinner dances commencing at 4:00pm. These dances were being sponsored by the student's union in support of the local pensioners to give back something to the community. The venture came about when the lady who was the manager of the Students Union Hall suggested to their committee, as a gesture of thanks to the past generation. Very noble a most appreciated and generous gesture which elevated the pensioners view of students, so often misconstrued and without justification.

This latest development left us to ponder how to reschedule our commitments to facilitate the extra requirement. Betty on studying the required dates saw that there didn't appear to be any occasions when the new project would clash with any other work. Therefore, no problems and after all, it would only be once a month.

By now I had a small but significant backlog of association work to be dealt with. This was mainly reading through various correspondence, signing cheques and documents. At national level the membership was increasing, and morale was at a very high level. I was also waiting for notification of the date and venue of the next NEC meeting, as I'd need to keep Betty informed so as not to let it clash with other commitments on her wall chart. We had been granted permission to erect a memorial in the National Memorial Arboretum, which is in Staffordshire. This was designed by one of the association members from the Doncaster branch, who by profession was a stonemason. Sadly, sometime later this had to be dismantled as the land we had been allocated was not fit for purpose. It would appear the land had not been properly drained. I have often thought of that true gentleman, mild mannered always polite and a fine craftsman. Sad to say that like so many of the founder members, he has been posted to those barracks above. God Bless.

The branch was gaining in strength and respect, both inside and outside the association. Before I move on to other things, it would be remiss if I did not refer to my very good friends John the secretary and Tom our treasurer. Stalwarts and backbone of the branch and on a personal level friends and comrades who were always as true as you would ever find. When working with them I was always relaxed and comfortable without that feeling of *"what's going on behind my back?"* They were the right men in the right place, at the right time. Giants among men.

I began to get a feeling that our chosen lifestyle was taking a more tranquil and enjoyable form. David now happy working for British Rail, with Fiona following in his footsteps to a degree. Her railway career including being the manager of the busy Travel Centre at Edinburgh Waverley station, before becoming the overall manager of Newcastle Central station. Betty and I were beginning to think about holidays. When the children were very young, we would holiday in Scotland and they were always full of fun and adventure. We would book a beach bungalow and spend some wonderful happy hours on the beach or go for long walks in the countryside. As I write this, a host of beautiful memories are recollected but the result of such memories, I have discovered in writing this book is heartbreak for the times you will never repeat. Thank God I'm alone, which I am grateful for. I think I would be well advised to take some time off now and return tomorrow, on I hope a lighter note.

So, to the time when I had to undertake quite probably the most high-profile of tasks, which at that time I thought was my misfortune to be confronted with. This was the installation of a memorial plaque in St Paul's Cathedral London. I must confess that at first, I was close to hitting the panic button. But I had my on-call tranquillizer. How could I ever manage without her?

Initially I needed to try and make contact with someone at the Cathedral, so to gather advice on the procedure for obtaining permission to hopefully make a successful application and have the plaque installed in the cathedral, to the memory of those who fell in the conflicts in Malaya and Borneo. Well good luck favoured me, as the very lady I was speaking to turned out to be my guide and mentor through this labyrinth of culture and history, until we ended up at a meeting in her office.

I established that her name was Vicky and her position was as the organiser of ceremonial events. She told me that I must first write to the Dean and Chapter who will decide if it is worth us proceeding any further. Behind all of this, we then had to submit our proposed design to the Fabric Committee for approval. One must note that the wording has to be appropriate and there are guidelines available.

I was asked if I had any questions and so I explained that we had a professional stone mason, who is well qualified and has himself created several works for other associations. Could we use him? I was informed that they would nominate a London based sculptor and my reaction to this was to think of how biased it seemed. It implied that they regarded northern craftsmen as inferior to London sculptors. I had to think quickly however and bear in mind that I had travelled here to try and achieve a lasting tribute to all those comrades of the British and Commonwealth Armed Forces, the Gurkhas and Malayan Security Forces who gave their lives in combat. I therefore chose to hold my tongue and try to keep my own counsel. I was sure to fail should I show any sign of retaliation. Discretion was the better part of valour.

There were other hills to climb, but they were miniscule by comparison. I must point out that the above was the only meeting where I attended on my own and all further negotiations were attended as a group, which usually also included our Patron. I took it upon myself to invite a small number of members who I considered well enough qualified to fill several positions to be supervised and these would be required for duty on the day of the event. It is only right that I should also make it clear that those invited to join this sub-committee, were from different branches. I made this decision to counter or dispel any suggestion of favouritism and there was only one member of my own branch.

A particular task I had to undertake, required me to break off from what in essence could have been covered earlier. But I had to hold it back to a meeting which was already imminent and which I felt was the best place to acquaint the sub-committee of the tragic demise of our National Treasurer. It came as I knew it would, a total shock to all. It was indeed so tragic. He was one of the younger members, which made it even more a tragedy. An all-round good chap, reliable, respected and loyal. God Bless You Godfrey we will always remember you.

I clarified with my sub-committee attendees, that they were comfortable with the duties I would like them to carry out on the run-up to and at the ceremony in the cathedral. I explained that it would be followed by a buffet reception hosted by the Lord Mayor of London. It would be very busy but rewarding in so much that in years to come, we could say that we made that event tick.

I did have further meetings at the Chapter House and on those occasions, I would be accompanied by the Patron and the Right Honourable DE who was an enormous help in attracting some very interesting and generous people to the cathedral.

I thanked the members of the sub-committee for their impressive performances and told them to hold themselves ready to attend one further with the Patron and me to wind things up.

Our next task was to launch a campaign to have the MOD expunge their referral to those who died in our conflicts as "non-war dead". Sir Garry Johnson, Bill Williams and I, met the Minister for Veterans Affairs at the Old War House in Whitehall. I am so pleased to say we won the day, but sad to say we were back once more shortly after, this time to help pursue the government to grant the Gurkhas and their families residence in the UK on completion of their service. This proves that achievements can be made by lobbying.

CHAPTER 12
Malaya – The Return

The next what I consider to be an outstanding event in my diary, is the long-awaited return to Malaysia. I had always promised Betty I would take her there some day and now the family were grown and flown, we had the freedom to go. We had a chance to travel with a group of veterans, so without further ado off we went to Penang. It was a fairly decent if long flight and I well recall on arrival at Penang airport the look on Betty's face when we left the aircraft to enter inside the airport building. She had a lightweight cardigan draped over her shoulders and a pleasant young customs officer smilingly said, "you will want to remove that when you step outside". He was referring to the extremely efficient air conditioning installed in the terminal. How right he was, for I had forgotten how powerful the outside heat was. We were then transferred by coach to our hotel.

Upon arrival, we were greeted by the staff and locals with garlands and a dance of welcome. We were treated with great warmth and affection and in the evening, we were invited to a dinner dance at the nearby Ton Jong Country Club, hosted by the local business community. I met a gentleman who was of Chinese Malay origin he and his wife were seated at the same table as Betty and me. As the evening went on there was dancing after the meal and our conversation progressed. It came across to me he was very interested in dancing and at one point even offering to pay our costs to go to Shanghai with his wife and him to enjoy the large number of dance halls in the city. I was a little more than inquisitive as regard his financial status, but the response appeared to be somewhat vague. It would seem he was wealthy, but no one was prepared to say how rich the gentleman was or what his line of business was. As I have never been a gambler, I politely declined his very generous offer and I am sure I had made the right decision and to this day do not regret it.

Before I move on, I have a confession to make. Perhaps I am flattering myself for I now have a picture in my mind of a growing sense of excitement that I am about to reveal my darkest secret - I don't like the west coast of Malaya. I by far prefer the east. Just my preference, but it was nearer to the cemetery at Batu Gajah where some of my colleagues were buried in what is now called Gods Little Acre. Bless, RIP.

There is not a great deal I would wish to say about this holiday. We took this one for cost and convenience and its inclusion of a trip to Batu Gajah. On the other hand, Betty was really enjoying it even though the sea was used as a rubbish dump with warnings not to go in. Fortunately, the hotel had a very large pool with a waterfall. The hotel was next to what had been the armed forces rest and recuperation centre, which was now the European school. It was there I along with a colleague spent my only period of leave in what was at that time three-day R&R. You see, even in those days I was such a lucky boy. The only change from those long-gone days was that the sea was clean and this time I was looking down on this scene from the balcony of my room on the 29th floor.

It was there and then I decided we would make our own holiday arrangements for the following year and we would head east. Soon it was time to go home, with the long and boring journey in front of us. Just sit back relax and dream of next year.

On our return to the UK it was so wonderful to see our children. They were both fine and there were lots of hugs from Fiona who might I say had developed into a bright and beautiful young lady. I can say that, it's what I call a father's privilege.

As one would expect, we just picked up from where we left off. The only difference was a reduction in the numbers attending the dances but being a former committee man, I knew it was all part of a pattern. There are two periods in a club calendar year that the numbers attending take a dip. They are the annual summer holiday time, along with January and February when quite often the weather can be just damned horrible to atrocious and add to that the fact most of those partaking are of the over 55 group. I would be lying if I said it never bothered us, for there were lots of times the weather put us off leaving the house, but we went and there was always the hardcore of our following present. We would always be available, to quote one of their favourites, *"Turn The Music Up"*. There was one thing I had overlooked, that being the monthly dance at the university. I refer to this because these are held during daylight hours and at a time when the roads and most of the pavements have been cleared. There are a substantial number who came by hired coach so I didn't anticipate that these would be a problem.

Having got the previous item passed and approved, which is the business side of our life it is time to move on. This would be to hold a meeting with John and catch up on association matters where both John and Tom had everything under control. I never for one-minute thought it would be any other. Top men, both myself and the membership were grateful that we had them in our team. Let me use an expression often used by some who do not understand the meaning of the phrase, they were truly loyal to the association and never backed away from a challenge. I like many others, did not realise their value in the work they carried out and their forethought in planning for the future. Bless them for their endeavour, a privilege and honour to have their friendship. Please do not misunderstand, they were not alone in their efforts for there were other very good men and women who were ready to step into the breach when required. I will not elaborate any further at the present moment, but I assure those who may have an interest in this period of time that I will never hold back on the acknowledgement of those who are prepared to go that extra mile to advance the development and creditability of the association. I know from experience several examples where a successful project has been delivered, only for the one who tasked or ordered someone else do the work then happily stand and accept any accolades that may be forthcoming. This is wrong and I cannot understand how they can live with that on their conscience.

I have had the honour and pride to hold high office over a period of some twenty years. In that time there have been highs and lows. The biggest low was the point where there was a massive probability the association would step out of existence, but for a few loyal men the NEC and with the support of some branches. We toughed it out and eventually shall we say, sailed into calmer waters. I'd rather not expand any further here on the nature of those challenging times.

At the Association reunion dinners, our president would amongst other things deliver his state of the reunion speech and at these events it was protocol for me to sit to the right of the president. That was until such precedence went out of the window and my wife Betty took my place. This made it easier to regale the president with some of her jokes. Sad to say, these times were all too short, for you will read a little later in the book my dear wife passed away.

There will be a full explanation in time, meanwhile I will continue to bring this present tale to a conclusion. So, from here I will return to the president's speech.

At the designated time he rose to his

feet and began his speech. He congratulated the officers and the NEC. He then turning to me said that he was so sad to be seeing me leave, as we had become friends and would remain as such to the end. He then went on to remind everyone in his own words, "if David had not fought the good fight, we could well have lost our association".

My response to the presidents very kind and complimentary remarks, was that they were both flattering and appreciated, but I would be remiss to take all the credit for what happened in those long previous stressful days. We must always remember that it was not just me. If anyone thinks that I had performed a worthwhile job, that would not be strictly correct. Yes, I was the National Chairman at that time and therefore the leader of the committee, but it is they who make the decisions. Always remember the chairman only has a casting vote and in almost 20 years in post I never had to use it. So, as I have said, they made the decisions and I am the one who delivers the poisoned chalice on occasions. One can take that as a play on words.

I was so fortunate to have such a strong dedicated and loyal NEC, and I must also include all those branches who gave us support and encouragement throughout the whole sad episode. Sad to say, it left a stain on some and in one instance a member died, so would never see the ending. RIP. It is nice to receive praise but be humble in receipt of it and always ensure credit goes too, to those who helped you achieve your successes.

National memories Kuala Lumpar, Malasyia

My favourite holiday, hotel at Kuantan

LAST MAN STANDING

I just feel it was necessary to clarify the procedure. When one is administering such as our association as it was in those days just about at its peak therefore things achieved at that time should not be attributed to one individual.

Compliments are very nice but soon blow away on the wind.

Therefore, I will revert to what must now be becoming almost like an exclamation mark, as I must use it so many times in such a long account of my journey through time. I will try to adhere to the relevancy to be economical with both time and space.

Almost a year had gone by, the family were grown and our small business was in good shape. So, Betty and I were making our arrangements to fly out to Kuantan for two weeks, in what I consider my idea of paradise. I was quite sure Betty would also fall in love with this spot, and after that very long but in the end rewarding journey, we arrived to that all too familiar Malaysian welcome. Amongst the welcome were some friends from the past, so wonderful to see once more, and the beginning of a wonderful time of rest and relaxation. Betty was totally overwhelmed by the beauty of the area, the beach of silver sand, the palm trees and the clean clear South China Sea. The first night we dined in what was known as the Kampung Restaurant. This is the largest of the four places to eat and served international dishes. For grills there was a small grill bar named Coals on the Beach where the food was cooked to order. We decided to try a different restaurant each night. Strange though it may be there was an Italian Bistro which was extremely good and very authentic but having over the years visited many such establishments, we both thought it had one outstanding feature. I am sure the question that leaps to mind is, *"what was the feature?"* Almost total silence. It was the quietest such establishment we have ever dined in. As the young ladies gracefully glided among the tables Betty said to me, they are so beautiful pleasant and efficient. As is the case in Malaysia they all speak English. On one occasion the girl who brought my bottle of Tiger I thanked in Malay, saying Teri-ma Kasai. She smiled, made a little curtsey and said, "sama sama!" She wished the same to me.

As I write this, I will say probably it was the most idyllic period of my entire life. My dream holiday spot with my dream girl, and we were being spoiled by an appreciative hotel staff who look upon you as a hero. That I feel was because I had been one of many who had served out there when their country was under threat. I have often thought since, what a pity it is that our own government could not show its own servicemen and women the same respect.

After all, there have been three very prominent conflicts which have taken place in the Far East since the end of the Second World War, of which the Malayan Emergency was the first. It is worth pointing out that the records may show its result was the largest number of casualties since the end of that world war, but the end resulted in victory for the British and Malayan Armed Forces, plus the Police and Commonwealth and in the vanguard the Gurkhas.

Therefore, to put this all-in context, the other conflicts were Korea and Vietnam. Taking these in perspective Korea was an armistice in other words a draw. I in no way would want to imply that our personnel involved were in any way lacking or failing in their performance. Quite the opposite, for it would be their outstanding tenacity that won so much admiration from their peers.

Vietnam was not our war. At the beginning it was a French campaign, who withdrew to allow the Americans to replace them. The outcome, yet another withdrawal that leaves one to ponder would our involvement have made a difference. I think such a situation would appear to bear similarities to Korea, where we would not be in overall command. I'm sure that if you asked a veteran from the Malayan campaign if this was a fair comment to make, they would concur, when one considers the outcome of that action. It is also well recorded that the only successful way to stand any chance of succeeding, was through hearts and minds. Be kind and be understanding, but also be in control. It worked for us and the proof is so evident, for on all of my visits to that land I have been met and made welcome by the locals, hotel staff and I even had a taxi driver declined my fare because as he put it, he would not have so good a life if it had not been for the British soldiers who brought peace to his country. And oh, we did win that one.

It may have come as a surprise to the

reader my little outburst, but by way of an explanation it has been festering in me for many years. I can only comment with any accuracy on the army, for I know little or none of the other services. I was a regular. In fact, at the time when I was serving, my regiment was the only all regular unit in the British Army. I therefore will try and enlighten you. In this so-called "emergency", as it ran its course from 1948 until 1960, over 1000 British troops were deployed. By far the majority were national servicemen. Sad to say, a considerable number never came home. Now in my mind, to those grieving families, that is a real emergency. Every man and woman who served out there knew it was war. The responsibility rests not only on the shoulders of the UK government at the time, but also all the successive governments since. One may well wonder how they can lie straight in their beds at night.

So for those who did not return, dear God look after them for their country did not and their sacrifice was demeaned by the fact they were classified "Killed in action". Perhaps it should be, "Fell in Protection of Insurance Company Interests". It is an insult to their memory and a lifelong heartbreak for their kind.

If I did not offload these feelings, which I have harboured for many years and take the opportunity to purge my mind of the horrific sights we had to witness. After that it was not very long before some of us would begin to think of the possibility of being captured by the enemy and the thought of what would happen prompted an imaginary club, that would activate what we would call be it jokingly "Save the last round for me" club. Thank goodness it was never put to the test. Here endeth my final lesson.

CHAPTER 13

Lost Loves

I was beginning to get weary from the constant rail travel to and from London but the outcome on all occasions was fruitful. This now left me with more time for Betty and home life. During this period, we managed to fulfil our dance obligations, except for one dance club night when I was on my way back from a meeting. However, my wonder woman ran this whole show and I have been told by some of my friends she did it with great expertise. I don't know who he is but if I get a chance to meet this Mr Expertise, I will most certainly soften his cough the dastardly cad.

After this period of rushing around hither and tither, we eventually settled down to what we consider to be a normal life, until the dark and cold winter evenings. Betty had an enormous dislike of fireworks and did not look forward to the 5th November, so I suggested we go away for the week covering that period. She questioned as to whether we be able to do that. I had though, for some time thought of retiring from running the dances, to enjoy some prime time to travel and feel free to do our own thing. We would have no restrictions if we end the dances. Once we had made our decision, I notified the club of our intention to withdraw our service. As I expected it was with a mixture of sorrow and gratitude on both sides and an open assurance that if we ever wished to return there would always be an open door for us.

I am sure this was the point good fortune deserted me. Knowing of Betty's aversion to Guy Fawkes night and the decision to go away at the time, we would call at the travel agents the following morning and see what was available. So off we went, so happy and still so much in love.

As one might expect, first port of call Eldon Square. Betty must do a tour of all the "fashion houses" therein. I was thinking to myself I must get my priorities right. She had almost completed her tour, with only one more to go her favourite and former place of employment Fenwick's. I had almost reached the point where I just had to have a cup of coffee and said to her "let's have a break", so headed for the patio cafe. She went and sat at a table and I went to get the coffee and scones. On my return she said, "Dave I can't move my left hand" and when I looked at her, I could see her mouth was out of shape.

The terrible reality dawned on me; she was having a stroke. I knew from when Betty worked there, they had a nursing sister on duty. I told Betty not to move until I can contact the sister, but she gave that idea a very strong thumbs down. I was by now getting very concerned. She asked me to take her to the car. I asked, "do you think I can manage that?" She said "if you love me you will".

So, we began our slow journey from the

basement in Fenwick's to level 10 in Eldon Gardens car park. To this day I don't know how we managed to reach the car, but we did. The RVI hospital was in the region of about 600yds from where we were. It was raining very heavily, and I had no option but to park in a restricted area and dash into the hospital. The lady at reception advised me that the hospital did not do Accident and Emergency. At this point I felt like I was about to explode, but then a Nursing Sister appeared from nowhere and quickly took control. I only wish I could have met that very efficient Nursing Sister later, to give her my grateful thanks (wonderful lady). A little later David arrived. He had been given the news via Christine his wife (who I'd managed to advise) and quickly got on the first available train from York, where he was working. By the way he was breathing when he arrived, I was more than a little concerned, but he assured me he was just out of breath as he had run all the way from the station. Then Fiona arrived and all the family were together gathered in what I took to be the day room. By this time Betty had been transferred to Newcastle General Hospital, we followed. After a short while a young doctor entered and said that he had come to explain what the cause of the stroke had been. Betty had a double brain bleed right side resulting in paralysis down her left side. He asked me for permission to operate. I advised him that this was my family with me, and I would like to confer with them regarding him carrying out the operation. I told the family that they should all be a part of this decision. The result from this was for him to go ahead and hope it would succeed. Well, sadly it didn't but she was still alive. I suppose I was the eternal optimist. So, it was time to pray and hope, but deep down I knew the party was over.

After some time, Betty returned home and I became her carer. This entailed me developing new skills, which involved so many things I had previously never expected to do. One must bear in mind that Betty was now paralysed and had to be lifted to do the most basic of things. I don't think I need to elaborate further. As you may well imagine there is always someone who is willing to advise you on how they would handle my situation, when you know damn well they have never been in this sort of position in their life. Irritating YES helpful NO BLOODY WAY. But such is life. I just held my tongue and kept my own counsel. We had to move into a bungalow, as the bathroom in our existing house was on the upper floor and so no longer easily accessible for Betty. So, we moved to Longbenton leaving behind what had been our home for the past 45 years and many friends, but when it comes to the well-being of your loved one. no challenge is too big. The sad thing is Betty had expressed her desire to buy a bungalow and here we were in a very nice one, but I would sooner have a healthy wife than a nice bungalow.

As I find writing this sad episode very heart-breaking and I beg the readers indulgence, for it is extremely difficult to focus on this present subject as memories come flooding back. I had to watch someone so beautiful begin to alter and then fade. My darling Betty, I will love you forever. I am sure many of you will think how dreadful, but it is not the end.

DAVID NEIL

Nine months later my beautiful daughter had an aneurysm and as I was taking care of Betty and unable to attend the hospital David had to deal with matters on my behalf. He had to call and advise me when the doctors had spoken him requesting consent to turn off the life support that was the only thing keeping Fiona breathing. She was too far gone. David's wife Christine, who is a nurse, assured me there was nothing that could be achieved by delaying the process. Therefore, it was all over. I don't think I have ever felt so inadequate in my life. I had to leave my son David to deal with this tragic situation, while I took care of Betty who had she been in good health, this would have most surely killed her. So, in a somewhat perverse way it was a blessing she was not her normal self.

There is a great deal I wish to say about my brilliant and talented daughter, but the power of emotion is still too strong despite the years that have passed since that awful time when we lost her. I find it so difficult to cope with the feelings, they are so prevalent. Therefore, the feeling of loss is inconsolable. I think there is no greater loss than the loss of one of your children. She had just celebrated her 44th birthday and was manager of Newcastle Central Station with a wonderful future in front of her. God Bless my little girl.

The above period and events were without a doubt the most difficult and painful item of penmanship it has been my misfortune to ever have to write, but I could not exclude them for they both are intrinsically part of this story. I can assure you that it has been quite a stress, so much so that I confess I had to leave it for a while, to regain some composure.

I had to settle myself to carry on in life and try to purge my mind of the darkest thoughts. But help arrived from an unexpected quarter and I suddenly realised I was not alone. I am now satisfied that what I needed to carry on, was someone to trust and if required give me a swift kick up the backside. Thank goodness, for this had to be the turning point after which I was befriended by two sweet ladies and as our friendships progressed. We would go out for lunch, or on some occasions have a trip away to my reunion dinners. We also did a VIP trip to the Royal Albert Hall to attend a John Wilson Orchestra concert. These two wonderful ladies so kind and so caring, always prepared to help out or chat on the phone and if I was having a bad day, they had an abundance of subjects to talk about or a matter to discuss, never beat for an answer or a joke. My good luck charms.

I now move on to yet another year, but life would be different now that I live on my own. Having said that, I must point out that I of course also have had the support of my family, their work time and other commitments permitting. At the time of writing, I have been in the Covid Pandemic lockdown and so visiting has been somewhat restricted. My immediate family have been my only visitors for much of this time, collecting and delivering my shopping and other requisites. I have therefore been a virtual recluse.

The problem this situation creates is that I do confess to being one who enjoys company and good conversation and if I am being totally honest, I am a bit of a spirited character when given the opportunity to be. This has on many occasions left me open to a fair amount of mickey taking by my fiends which I don't mind in the least for I am more than capable of retaliation. More often than not, with a touch of humour. In my opinion, there is nothing more amusing than a light-hearted what I think of as verbal jousting, providing it is conducted in a spirit of banter.

I shall now be thinking back to the story which I feel I was obliged to digress from as it had suddenly dawned on me the biggest part of the book occurs in the past tense. I hope this makes sense.

I neglected to mention earlier that when my wife fell ill, I took the decision to stand down from office with the NMBVA. This I did to be with and nurse her in my misguided idea that it would help her back to full health. I quickly realised however, that was never going to happen. I did not want to have her placed in a care home and resisted any attempt to let people go over my head. My resistance was both vigorous and unyielding, but sadly after over two years of loving care and devotion, I had to concede as my own health was in jeopardy and so off she was sent. I won't name the establishment in which she was placed, but I will say that I feel her treatment was somewhat inadequate. Due to my state of health I needed to concentrate on getting myself back to something like better fitness. I had lost a great deal of weight and had almost forgot about the luxury of a full night's sleep. Therefore, it was during this period that a member of the nursing staff somehow managed to have Betty referred and transferred to a mental facility. On my insistence we had her moved to a much better care home, more suited to her condition. It was here that my darling had a further stroke and was moved to the RVI hospital, where she never regained consciousness. In the early hours of a beautiful sunny June morning the time 5:15am she slipped away, and I like to think the birds were singing her on her way. Our loss is Gods gain. Bless you sweetheart, we will meet again, not too long now.

From thereon in, I have lived on my own and it appears that is how my life is to be, until I spin off this mortal coil. It is also a time to assess who of the people I associated with, were real or just acquaintances. To me, a real friend is the one you can depend upon. An acquaintance comes in many categories. Some who you can trust in all matters, reliable, helpful and loyal. There are some who think they might gain from the appearance of being regarded as part of our company, click or gang. They were I think false or insincere, not the genuine article and best avoided if possible.

In closing this, may I say in hindsight and reflecting on all the various people who have travelled this long journey with me throughout this very varied trip from joyful holidays at my aunts in Kent to joining the army and my time with the regiment of my choice.

Travelling with my regiment through those early years of the Malayan campaign, a period of many contrasts. From action and excitement, to boredom and frustration. Witnessing sights of outstanding beauty and of unbelievable cruelty and I myself suffered combat injuries. But, through it all I had my largest group of friends standing shoulder to shoulder with me yes, my Band of Brothers. With the information I have at time of writing, it appears that I am the last man standing. So, adhering to the troops unwritten rule book, I will install myself in the departure lounge and await my impending RTU. I must confirm to the reader I am not a damn misery; I just don't want to be here any longer to run the risk of creating problems for my family and dear friends.

As I sit here to once more write this book, I reflect on my frustrations. I am nearing the end of this project, during which I've experienced unhelpful periods of health problems, of tiredness and all very difficult to control. Then it has been further exacerbated by the COVID-19 pandemic, and the restrictions that have been imposed to try and eradicate this. I pray to God for my family and friends, that they will survive this dreadful pandemic sweeping the entire world, leaving in its wake a trail of death and heartache. To the Lord, I pray please set us free from this situation.

As time has moved on, I have though been able to retrieve my composure and perspective. I only achieved this with the help, guidance and encouragement, from my son, his family and my dear friends, among them those two exceptionally outstanding ladies. Their encouragement and compassion have helped me revive my flagging spirit. So, with this support I knew I just had to go on if for no other reason than to not let my son and family down. Both he and my friends were pushing me to stand again for National Chairman of the NMBVA at the forthcoming AGM. Combined with this, I was now receiving by email and phone, pledges of support from a considerable number of branches and many individuals to return to office. My reaction was that this was to all intent, rather ego boosting. But contrary to what others may think, that is not my style although at times I may appear that way. It would be that only when placed in a situation, I may then be required to adopt a stance that gives perhaps the false impression. I am a great believer in loyalty, discipline and protocol. I enjoy a little social banter, but only if it's inoffensive humour.

Therefore, after due consideration I decided to go for it. Time came and went, and I found myself back as chairman. I had a new NEC with vice-chair secretary and treasurer. My branch secretary Val also joined the NEC, which was a substantial saving for the association. Living quite close, Val would travel with me being picked up and dropped off at the doorstep. I began to settle in, quietly assessing the members of the NEC who I did not know too well. If there was some sort of problem, I would rather talk with him or her and try to understand whatever the cause may be. I can't rectify whatever is wrong if I am not aware of the would-be problem.

How is it that there is inevitably always someone of the kind that when the likes of I speak, their facial expression is a portrayal of what must be going on in their mind? There was a case in point during this time. I often ponder as to why this person behaved in such a manner. If I had offended him, I had not realised. But not to say anything? Whatever it was, I am sure I would have had it out with him, although I feel I can hear a certain someone not all that far away from me uttering "yes indeed you would big mouth". As it happens, the gentleman in question has sadly passed away and so I'll never know. Pity, as I thought that I was approachable. You live and learn.

A Light in the Darkness – Ruth

After the loss of my wife and daughter, as you may well imagine my spirit was at an all-time low. I know I was withdrawn and reclusive and only ventured out for life's necessities. I was never a great TV fan, but as fate had decreed one Saturday evening, I was prompted to switch on what I refer to as the haunted fish tank. The BBC were showing the proms from the Royal Albert Hall, featuring the at that time emerging and nowadays renowned John Wilson Orchestra. Well, being a music lover, I was quickly captivated by the sight, sound and production of this cultured and obviously talented collection of musicians that you would find difficult to replace anywhere in this world.

There are some who may find it hard to understand how this affected me, and almost launch me on my journey of rehabilitation to a

*new life. And adding to this, it there was the
creation of a most wonderful friendship with a
member of that outstanding musical dream. Her
name Ruth Rogers, a remarkable gifted violinist
and may I say beautiful lady. She now has two
very bright and talented young boys and in
overall command, Ruth's husband Tom. God Bless
them all.*

Around this time, I started to think
about some advice given to me by my son David,
although initially by just saying "oh yes I
will get around to it someday". His advice was
I should get away for a while, maybe enjoy a
relaxing trip back to Malaysia for two or three
weeks. As I say, I was a bit dismissive at
first, but I noticed that a lot of my friends
were offering me the same advice. Almost word
for word. It dawned on me that I was being
brainwashed in a concerted effort to send me
off on my own. Well that is not strictly true,
for I had several old friends and knew a good
number of police officers in Kuantan area,
where I would wish to go. I somehow had this
feeling or picture set in my mind as to how it
would be in Kuantan, when all the troubles were
over. Well it certainly did not follow my idea
of how it would look now. So, it was time to
succumb to the brainwashing and book up for two
weeks at the Kuantan Hyatt Regency. I'd be on
my own, but then I only had myself so could do
as I please. I would take this opportunity to
visit our graves and place poppy crosses on the
headstones and also I'd meet up with some old
friends and visit the new out of town police
HQ. I was made aware of this by my good friend
at the High Commission Office Nick Reece (Royal

Just good friends

Me with Ruth
and Brenda

Ruth – John Wilson   Me and Ruth
Orchestra Violinist

Me with Alexander and Oliver, Ruth's boys

Malay Police Special Branch).

I would be less than honest if I were to say that I was not excited at the prospect of returning to Kuantan. I look upon it as my second home. Sadly, it was the first holiday I went alone and my first trip on KLM Schiphol to Kuala Lumpur. By a strange quirk of fate on boarding the aeroplane, it was a Boing 747 and as frequent travellers will know the layout of the seating is rows of three on each side of economy class (with a row of four in the centre). My seat was about halfway down port side. I had the outside seat; the inside seat was occupied by a young Malaysian lady. She greeted me with what I recall a typical warm smile and I was thinking how it would be a pity for someone to come along at the last minute and occupy the middle seat, depriving me of some pleasant conversation on such a long journey. Then two things occurred in quick succession. First, we were taxiing for take-off and the offending seat had not been occupied, then, it very soon turned dark and after a meal the lights were lowered to enable passengers to get some sleep. Those who are familiar with this mode of travel, will know that on long haul flights passengers each have a lightweight blanket to assist in providing a more comfortable sleep. At the point when everything dimmed down, the young lady asked if I would mind if she had the spare blanket off the unoccupied seat, as she was cold. Being the gentlemen that I would hope to be, I told her she was more than welcome. As a result of this, we had a most welcome little interlude which began with introductions. She told me her name

212

was Zemar, that she was a manager of a Malaysian Tour Company and her office was in KL. She was returning from a conference in Berlin. I told her that I was a veteran of the emergency going back to visit my former playground, but also to pay my respects at the final resting place of my comrades we had to leave there. The dear girl was very moved and told me that she had the deepest and sincerest respect for those brave young men who made that long journey to establish freedom for her homeland. I thanked her for such kind and beautiful words, thanking her also on their behalf too. She replied that she should be saying those words to me, for I had been there when this all took place and she was told by her parents of some of the cruel things inflicted on the nation in those years by the CT's.

On our arrival at KL airport, it was time for us to go our separate ways. She to take the airport express train into the city and home, I to board the driverless train across the airport to the domestic flights' terminal, for my flight to Kuantan. Being that the airport was so large, my charming new friend insisted she accompany me to my new departure lounge before she went home and so before she left, we had one more cup of coffee. Over that drink, she promised to drive over to visit me on the following Saturday, and so she did. That friendship has never ended and two years later we met up once more when I was visiting with my granddaughter Kate and she had somehow got us in the penthouse suite in a luxury hotel, for the one night we were stopping over in KL. Kate had a wonderful time and I think she too fell in love with Malaysia.

So, returning to this trip, and so it seems to have been a wonderful quirk of fate that brought about that meeting of two total strangers, who just appeared to gel and in a matter of twelve hours, became true friends despite the vast difference in ages. She respected both I and my comrades and I reciprocate in kind.

Moving on from this pleasant encounter, hopefully to enjoy the remainder of the holiday. What I think of as a commitment, was my visit to Police HQ. So, I rang them to establish what would be the most convenient time to call. I received an assurance that I could if I wish, be collected from the hotel. If this would be the preferred option, ask the hotel to inform the HQ and a car would be sent to get me. So, I asked the hotel staff if they were alright to oblige, which they were. Much to my and the hotel reception staff surprise, when I took a casual stroll to reception, it appeared to be unusually busy for that time of day. Most of those present were a mixture of foreign tourists, predominately I would say Asian who were very loud, but on my appearance fell silent. As I took a step into the main area, I quickly knew the reason behind this rather spectacular assembly. Oh dear, it must be little old me. My friend the hotel concierge manager came to my aid. At the desk were two Royal Malayan Police, a captain and a sergeant prepared to take me into HQ. There were signs of disappointment on many faces when I extended my hand toward them, as I'm sure the crowd thought they were going to cuff me whereas we shook hands. This was followed by what I would call a pregnant pause while the penny dropped, and everyone had a good laugh at their own expense. We then drove off to HQ. On arrival, a very warm welcome awaited me. It is this very outgoing display of appreciation and respect that I feel draws me to the Malaysians. They are a very cheerful people and it is always a joy to have their company.

I must confess, I was really tempted to take up the offer of the Malaysian Government to participate in the Malaysia My Second Home (MM2H) scheme. This was an offer both attractive and sincere. There would be no question of loneliness for I had many friends out there. But my birthplace is Tyneside and that is where I wish to end my days, back in England, my home, my pride and land of my family for many centuries. I like Malaya so very much, but my love of my homeland exceeds all others and so I will end my days at the spot where my family can see me off. By the way, I told David that when I go no expense is to be spared, get two bags of crisps.

I suppose you might be thinking, *"oh, he has wandered off again"*. That's me, the Master of Digression or in memory circles better known as the Happy Wanderer.

Returning to the story and the Malaysia trip, my visit to Police HQ turned out to be quite enlightening as to how the workings of a very new up to date 21st century Police HQ functions. I then had tea with the commander

and arranged to have a tour of the outstations.
This would entail a trip to Sungai Lembing,
where Mr & Mrs Black had lived. How I wish
Bill was with me now. So, after our plans were
put in place, I was driven back to the hotel
for dinner and a good night's sleep. The next
morning, I was up had breakfast and all set
to hit the road for the first of many what I
can only describe as sentimental journeys. And
this first was I think the most prominent of
all, rekindling fond memories of now long-gone
days and two of the most wonderful people it
has been my honour and privilege to be able
to say were our friends. Much to my delight
in Sungai Lembing, there is a small museum
dedicated to the now defunct mine and the
British compound and there in that very museum
in a room adorned with photographs, were our
friends Mr & Mrs Black from the days when they
were newly married.

Over the next seven days, I was escorted
to every police station or post in East Pahang.
I must say, I thoroughly enjoyed every mile and
minute and for most of the time we travelled at
my request on the old roads, which allowed me to
absorb the true atmosphere. Along the way, we
called at once familiar places such as Gambang,
Maran, Bentong, Kuala Lips, Raub and Trass. I
must confess, this particular episode of my
travels were the most relaxing and refreshing,
with my appointed driver Silver, by name and
also by quality. We truly enjoyed each other's
company. He was very knowledgeable and well
read. Even though he was not born at the time
of the conflict, his father had been involved.
He also possessed a very British sense of

humour. His origins were Malaysian Indian, and he explained that his father had worked as a Forest Ranger. When the country was overrun in 1941, his father went into the jungle and joined Force 136. He remained with them until the end of hostilities. If that is so well done that man.

It was all too quickly approaching the time to return to the UK. I had very mixed feelings regarding the imminent departure. I truly wanted to stay, but I decided to go home to Geordieland. And the fact is, I don't regret it one iota. On the day before leaving, Jo the assistant concierge invited me to his home for dinner that evening, which was a big surprise. On the day of my departure, Silver was sent to take me to the airport for the flight to KL. On arrival in KL, sad to say I had a four-hour layover. There is little that is more time consuming and totally frustrating than spending time in an airport. They are basically uncomfortable, unfriendly and the food and shops are grossly overpriced. I'm assuming that most readers will have had a similar experience at some time or another. As I sat, it occurred to me there are boxes hanging from the ceiling containing a human voice, which at irregular intervals tells you what you can do, or more often informs you what you can't do. Like get a flight that's on schedule sometimes without a number. This is what happened to me. A word to the wise, if you find yourself in an airport and you see me standing in line, go to another line. That is unless you happen to be a masochist and join me. You probably not get what you want and by hell you'll suffer.

So eventually I arrived home and regrettably I was suffering from jet lag, the only occasion that this has affected me. Perhaps a result of advancing age and bad temper, two facts I am not proud of but alas it goes with the territory. This thought and all it implies, more than it indicates that I am more than just a grumpy old man. As a popular song said, *"it's very nice to go travelling but it's so much nicer to come home".* The first major task is to get my washing sorted then sweet talk someone into ironing it for me. Failing that I will have to do the job myself. These are the times when you realise, you're not as popular as you thought.

With everything in order at home it was approaching time to attend an NEC meeting. I would collect Val from her home to travel with me, thus saving her having to get a bus or a train and she was a good travel companion. This made the journey pleasant for she knew when it was appropriate to speak, when to remain quiet and when to hold some sort of relevant conversation. In all she made some of these often long a potentially boring trips more tolerable, laughable in a way, for on many things we were poles apart but being a perfect gentleman and modest, would always concede to the lady.

I was happy to see that in my absence; the association had continued to progress and prosper. However, there was now a decline in numbers notable, be it all very slight by that point. It would therefore be advisable to quietly monitor this trend, which I would undertake so as not to activate any alarms. For if it was picked up by someone else, they could put their own interpretation on the issue and the rumour factory goes into overdrive causing untold problems and that in turn leads to misunderstandings.

As I write this, my thoughts go back to some five or six years earlier. It concerned me then, as I became aware of the intricacies of terminating an organisation, which are quite complex and precise. When I attempted to persuade my colleagues to investigate the matter, I got the distinct impression that I was talking to myself. It was then that I began to think I was losing any power of persuasion I may have possessed, and it might be time to give some thought to retiring. If as a leader you can no longer advise or inspire your colleagues, you are no longer a leader and you run the risk of becoming a subject of ridicule. So, it was it seemed, time to prepare my exit. I know along with a small number of former members who were prepared to stand with me in what I will call the early turbulent years of the Association, which resulted in a heavy impact on them both financially and health wise that was a high price to pay to keep the association evolving. Wherever those old friends are now God bless and eternal gratitude for your unfailing and truly inspiring loyalty and devotion.

I vowed at the beginning of this book not to use real names, except in a few cases such as those who gave me their permission. Otherwise however, my vow has applied, and I will make it clear here that this applies to both friend and foe.

To conclude this item, it is by way of an explanation as to why I feel that I have fulfilled my commitment to the membership, of whom there will be many not aware of these matters for it all took place before they joined us. I do not look for accolade but give some thought to that NEC of 1998 to 2003.

Having now decided in view of my rapidly advancing years and my declining health, could it be I am now not fit for purpose or surplus to requirements? This is not me being negative about the situation, I would like to think just plain honest. Not once but twice I was encouraged to don the mantel of responsibility. Now I would be among the first to admit how I was uncertain but flattered that branch members looked upon me as being capable of fulfilling that position, on both occasions. However, on reflection one wonders. Apart from many of my local branch officers and members, there are few in the association who know of me or my service to the cause. Therefore, and facing reality, I must face the fact in the final analysis, there are very few who want to know yesterday's man.

Is there a lesson to be learned from all this? Well, don't join if you can't take a joke. Have I achieved anything at all from all of this? Yes! There would not be an association today if I and a handful of dedicated men, had not stood up to defend the very existence of the Association. I cannot be sure, but I may be the last man standing of those truly loyal and devoted men and their families.

CHAPTER 14

The Journeys Continue

Once more it is time to move on and as promised, I will now fulfil what I wrote much earlier in this book, when I said that we had not heard the last of my good friend Bill. At the time I write of, Bill was living not too many miles away from me. I regret to say, that he since passed away several years ago. But for several years, we shared some very happy and exciting times. Like myself, Bill had also lost his wife. I am sure you would understand how with us having been friends going back over sixty years, it was quite natural to extend and develop that friendship into our everyday life. And that is exactly what happened. If I was attending a meeting, he often would accompany me and on occasions take a trip away to somewhere interesting or visit an event. We always would meet every Wednesday in the Patio Cafe of Fenwick's Department store on Northumberland Street, in my fair city of Newcastle upon Tyne, cherished and beautiful and home of St James Park a shrine to all Magpies. You'll find the folk *"nowt but canny"*. May I indulge with a short quote from my poetry book More Reflections, *"To be a Geordie is so fine born on the banks of the River Tyne"*.

So, the next event on this journey through life centres around my friend Bill and I deciding to go on a cruise. We pondered long

and hard and eventually decided on two weeks
in the Caribbean. Our hosts the Thompson Dream
cruise ship. We took a flight from Newcastle to
Barbados, where we were transferred to the ship
and sailed on the evening tide for what I could
only describe as pure bliss. Fine weather and
calm seas resulting in a good night's sleep.
I rose early, cup of tea, showered, dressed
and met Bill on the boat deck. Once around the
ship then breakfast. As we were at sea all that
day, everything was conducted in a very orderly
yet relaxed way. Bill and I had struck up a
friendship with a member of the crew his name
was Alves. He was Filipino, as were most of the
ship's crew and he was a leading light in the
crew's concert party. Among other features of
this most extremely well organised trip were
several ports of call. Bill and I did not take
part in any of these trips. Friends we had
made on the voyage would ask why we did not
indulge. Our reply among other things was that
we enjoyed the tranquillity on board the ship,
once the "*common people*" as we jokingly put it,
had gone ashore. We did what we came for "*to
chill out*".

We also befriended the resident pianist,
to such an extent that when the time came
to return home, he came to see me before I
disembarked. I had given him a copy of my poetry
book Reflections, the proceeds of the sale of
this book going to the Gurkha Welfare Trust
(GWT). I had given him a copy as a gift and was
not attempting to sell it to him. He said he
realised that, but still wished to donate to
the cause. I thanked him and assured him that
the money would go to the GWT just as soon as

LAST MAN STANDING

I got home.

The flight back to Newcastle was a night flight. We had paid a supplement and had meals and drinks but, in all honesty, I think we slept most of the journey and arrived ahead of time. Needless to say, what a transformation from tropical sun to dreary grey skies, but we both agreed much better than a troop ship.

We were collected from the airport by David my son and we took Bill home first. On the way we arranged to meet in the patio cafe in Fenwick's at 11:00am the following Wednesday. And so, to home for a meal, go through the mail, emails and phone calls and then off to bed.

So, it is once more a return to normal routine. As I have indicated in the past, the only downside about holidays is the problem of unpacking washing and ironing as when this has been completed, I feel like I need another holiday.

There was one pleasing aspect, a sharp fall in the amount of mail and messages awaiting me. Have we become so efficient with the other officers dealing with the queries, so as not to bother me? Or perhaps they don't like the response they get from me. That will only be revealed at the next AGM, which was still some time off.

So as there appeared to be very little ongoing association business that would involve me, I took advantage of this quiet period to pay attention to some domestic and personal matters. This would ensure that at times when

I am not at home, everything was kept in good order. It also allowed me some prime time with the family and very closest friends, for they all mean so very much to me. That whole group have been essential to my very existence over the past few years. They held me together when I was in danger of falling apart.

I always keep in mind those who have sustained me through some mind destroying years of my life and are still there to give me some often-required solace, companionship and a reason to live. And this I hoped to do along with my friend Bill. We discussed the prospect of going away a little earlier than we normally do and so planned to visit our travel agent on our weekly trip into town. Two days later, I received a phone call from Bill to tell me that he had visited his local branch of our favourite travel shop and picked up two copies of the cruise brochure. He asked if it would be alright if he come over to go through them and try to find a cruise, we would both enjoy. It may save time if we gained an idea about what would be best for us. Then I received a phone call from Val. It was on association matters, but I mentioned to her that Bill was with me and we were planning a cruise for next year. She was a little more than just interested I would suggest, and she asked us to keep her informed. So, by the time we got everything sorted out it looked as though there would be three of us for this high sea adventure. So, hoist the Jolly Roger the deadly trio are about to set sail.

The following week I met Bill in Newcastle

at our usual watering hole, for our regular coffee with cream and a portion of ham and egg pie. Then off up Northumberland Street to the Lunn Poly travel agency to book our cruise in the Mediterranean, on the same ship as before, the Thompson Dream. Naturally it was great to be reunited with some members of the ship's crew. Bill and I made some alterations in our dining arrangements from our previous cruise, in so much as we had breakfast on the sun deck, lunch on the lido deck, but for dinner we truly went upmarket and frequented the Orion Restaurant. In truth we only went there because our crazy friend from our previous cruise Alves was now working on that station. My thoughts were that if you are of a nervous disposition then you best get off at the next stop, for the rest of the incumbent staff were just as barmy as Alves. At the completion of service, they would put on a display of unreserved madness that could be found anywhere on the high seas. Believe it or not this performance occurred every evening of the voyage. All the waiters and other dining room staff appeared to be involved. We always tried to leave late so that we could enjoy the full show.

Just a brief outline of how we occupied our time. The general idea was everyone would do their own thing, so Val who in my eyes was something of an adventurer would go ashore to visit the port, or sometimes go on one of the organised trips. Bill and I preferred to stay and spend our time onboard to enjoy a little liquid refreshment, a good meal at lunch time and have a chat with some of the crew, or some of the other passengers who like us did not have any desire to indulge in any form of exercise or the like. Bill and I had figured that the time was now long gone to expend any further energy, after the large amount spent for King and Country in the stinking jungles of Malaya.

Then it was time for home. For Val and I there would be the usual mail, emails, phone calls to answer and often meetings to attend. Oh yes, and bloody washing and all that it entails. Each time I reach this point I vow I will never go away again!!!

I received a reminder from "Sir" that we were now approaching the anniversary of the St Paul's NMBVA Memorial dedication service. It had been suggested that we hold a service and combine it with the 15th anniversary of the ending of hostilities in Borneo. On this occasion, the planning was arranged in a much different way. An outside company in conjunction with the National Secretary took on responsibility for accommodation, catering and transport. I assisted the National Secretary, Ted Williams, in acquiring a detachment of Gurkha's for ceremonial duties. There was also a piper from Tyneside branch. Once the service was over, we moved to the Mansion House for a buffet reception to round off a memorable day. There was no requirement for a large number of ushers, as they were provided by the Cathedral. In closing this summary of the event, I would like to extend my delight and gratitude to Lady Sarah and Lady Anna (widow of our former patron). Regrettably time and duty left me little time to have a chat, but that's the way these occasions go. And to close, two more outstanding personalities who gave a truly magnificent performance those being Ted and Val.

Went the Day Well!

As I bid farewell to so many friends to begin my train journey back to Newcastle, I had time to ponder as to how much longer I would wish to do all of this travelling, attending meetings and various other associated events that were part and parcel of the job. I wasn't getting any younger, approaching the big 90 and I was also aware of my declining health. I remained fully focussed, but I was getting increasingly tired and I am sure that by now I didn't owe the association anything. Perhaps if I put my name forward to stand for one more year!

Therefore, it was time to start planning for my withdrawal within the next eighteen months and that would only be at national level. Whilst I could, I would not wish to forgo my membership of my beloved Tyneside branch. It is as well to remind you that I am writing this whilst in isolation and lockdown. You may consider how I chose to make my arrangements so far in advance. I could never be portrayed as having remarkable foresight. Had I possessed such ability, then I would probably have avoided the problems I encountered in the early days of my time in office.

There was an NEC meeting coming up where I would make my intentions known to the committee and see if someone would care to take on the post. Come the day, they all sat around the table in silence, some looking at some paperwork others gazing at the ceiling. This I must confess left me asking myself whether anyone wanted to take the job. I did detect however, one member whose expression indicated to me that he may not himself put forward for the position, but he perhaps had someone in mind who he could nominate. Then, if they were successful, they would be able to shall we say pull the strings, no doubt to the advantage of who helped them get there. I will not elaborate more, but it was sometime later that he let it slip on a social occasion that this was his intention, which only confirmed that my suspicion had been spot on.

This is not some form of portrayal of how clever I am. During my early years as chairman, there had been some torrid times that I and others had to endure. We were subjected to quite lengthy periods of questioning by a variety of investigators, solicitors and court officials. So somewhere along the way, I think that perhaps I picked up one or two tricks.

Life went on until the deadline for nominations for the committee were due to close. When a dear friend asked me to stand for one more year, I somewhat reluctantly agreed. The vote went my way, so there I was with one more year to do.

Having realised that I was now on the wrong side of the hill I would have to tailor my life accordingly. Part of this was to fulfil a long overdue promised trip back to Malaysia with my darling granddaughter Kate, but first

LAST MAN STANDING

I had to establish when she would be able to go to which I received a very prompt reply. It would appear she was quite enthusiastic. So, it was now time to make all the arrangements and contact my friends and some of the staff at my hotel. I was so happy to be having my very clever girl with me on this occasion. I just wanted to make this a holiday to remember.

I went ahead and arranged our flight to KL then onto Kuantan which would be our base for fourteen days. I had already contacted my friend Joe the Concierge Manager, who told me to send him our arrival time and he would collect us from the airport at Kuantan. So, all that was left to do was to pack and prepare. That would be more complicated for Kate than for me. She is a reincarnation of her grandmother Betty, an out and out *"clothesaholic"*. She reminds me in so many ways of my darling Betty.

Well, at last the day of departure arrived. Christine came to pick me up and take us to the airport for our 13.30 departure. Check-in and security were no problems, a smooth take off and a long journey ahead of us. It was a good flight, cabin staff were very attentive, service and food quite good and all-round a pleasant trip.

On arrival at KL we did not have to collect our luggage as it was booked through to Kuantan. We had about an hour's wait before boarding our Kuantan flight, a 50-minute trip. After arriving at Kuantan, I could see Joe waiting for us, but by some quirk of fate our luggage had not been put on the flight at KL. As it was now getting late, Joe got hold of the airport duty manager and delivered a good old Malayan rant. Joe informed me that our luggage would be at our rooms in the morning. This sorted, we got into Joe's car and headed for the hotel. There was a funny little occurrence of note on our way, let me explain. Kate has travelled quite extensively in European Countries and America and as we went along, she leaned over and whispered, "Parpar, Joe's driving on the same side of the road as we do at home". I explained that this was a former British Colony and almost all such countries have kept things that way. I added that, "wherever we have been, we have always left a footprint. That's why your Parpar and friends had to come out here to prevent it falling into the wrong hands. I hope to take you to my place of pilgrimage while we are here, and we will make our plans tomorrow after a good night's sleep".

As Joe had promised us on the night of our arrival, as in we arrived but our luggage didn't, thanks to his negotiating technique our cases were at our room doors when we got up the next morning. As we were in the Regency Club rooms, in our breakfast lounge you help yourself and a young lady would serve you tea or coffee. During our meal we discussed what Kate would like to do. I was not in the least surprised when she said she would very much like to have a relaxing day by the pool and that was not a problem, as there were three to choose from. One had a bar with in-pool stools. I thought this may be her preferred choice, as it is on hand for a refreshing drink, handy for the Kampung restaurant for lunch and to this young lady above all else, it was right beside the hotel shop. I said, "yes why not." She paused and said, "probably best to go in the pool now whilst the sun is out". I could not help it, for I laughed and told her at this time of the year it will be up there until it goes down. "How do you know that?", she asked. I replied that, "it's all arranged, I have influence, see you at the pool", and off I went for a cold Tiger.

It was not long before she appeared in her bikini. I had already asked the pool attendant to put her beach towel on her lounger and she said that she may try a dip in the sea later in the day.

I had chosen this time of year to come because the Malaysian children were at school, so the hotel and places of interest were much more visitor friendly.

To return to my darling Kate, she spent a considerable time in or by the pool on the first day. We had a light lunch in the Kampung restaurant and after lunch she had a look in the hotel shop. Then about 4pm we went to our respective rooms to cool down in the air conditioning. Then it was a shower and dress for dinner, which we would have in the Italian Bistro. This was very nice, so much so we both decided we would dine there every evening. Matt the Chef was a friend of many years as were lots of the staff. Each day Matt would contact me to ask if there was any particular dish Kate and I may like. He would then prepare them for the following evening meal. I asked Kate if she was ready for a new adventure and said I would introduce her to my driver in the morning, who will take us to wherever we wish to go. She said, "that sounds great". So, I asked my friend Joe to make the arrangements for 09.30 in the morning. After dinner that evening, we went for a stroll along the beach ending up in the San Pan bar. This place is quite unique. It was originally used by refugees escaping from Vietnam, ending up washed onto the beach right where it is now. The Malaysian authorities were about to burn it down when the hotel owners said they would buy it, which was agreed. It was placed on a bed of concrete and refurbished as a beach bar. I am sure we had a drink then the short walk back to our respective rooms, to meet in the breakfast lounge next day.

After a good night's sleep, it was breakfast and up to reception to meet my driver Silver. He has taken care of my transport requirements for several years now. His qualities are many and varied which include politeness, punctuality, extremely safe and respectful to other road users, and he is well versed in local and national knowledge. A truly intelligent fellow and a pleasure to have him in your company. I always looked forward to meeting him whenever I visited Kuantan.

I introduced Kate to Silver, and he asked then where we wished to go. I suggested the Sultans Palace at Pahang and the surroundings. It is picturesque and historical. Kate said that would be fine and off we went. Silver always had a good stock of bottled water in a cool box, an essential in these temperatures.

LAST MAN STANDING

We had an interesting and informative day, returning about 3:00pm for Kate to have some time in the pool before dinner. My friend Joe came and asked if we would like to have dinner at his home the following evening. This was not unusual; it had become a regular event on my trips to Malaysia. His wife would prepare dinner and we would be joined by their children and some members of his family. On all these occasions, Joe would collect and return us to the hotel. Naturally we accepted but, on this occasion, there was an amusing little interlude. It turned out that Joe's niece, who is the same age as Kate hit it off from the start. After our meal and whilst we were enjoying coffee Kate and her new friend went missing only to reappear a little later, with Kate adorned with a Hijab the Malay traditional ladies head dress. This provided some amusement for an hour or so, then it was time to leave. They are so friendly and kind.

The following day we went into town to enable Kate to visit the shopping centre but returned to the hotel for lunch and to relax with a Tiger beside the pool. At this point I have just realised that I have not mentioned the Regency Club area of the hotel. This is the upgraded part of the establishment. It is quiet, with attentive staff who are highly trained in amongst other things, Wi-Fi. On this occasion and as part of an international training programme, there happened to be two very lovely young ladies from Nepal, also about the same age as Kate. They were on the training programme. The routine was: breakfast, light lunch and early evening cocktail before dinner in one of the other restaurants. Well quite often Kate and I would go in after our evening meal to have a chat with the staff when we were the only ones about, but this developed into a regular event. I think the girls loved to talk with Kate and along with them we had some truly amusing times, all in very good taste. There was one little anecdote however, I thought deserves a place in this book. It goes like this. Kate always refers to me as Parpar. Well those two little darlings Rena and Prishanta, began to do the same. Now as it happens, there was a German couple in the Regency Club. I and possibly others considered them to be very rude to the staff. I was on my way to thank Joe, his wife and family and so was walking along the pathway, when I realised that the ill-mannered German couple had come out of their room and were following me a short distance behind. I had developed a rather low opinion of them and had I been on my own as I had been on previous trips, then I would not have restrained from confronting them. But I did not wish risking a scene when I had Kate with me, so that was ruled out. But to continue, as I walked along, I saw the two little darlings Rena and Prishanta coming towards me both carrying their schoolbooks. They spotted me and began to run to greet me shouting Parpar and putting their arms around me. Oh my God! The look on the Jerries faces. I often wondered what was going through their minds. Perhaps it was coincidence or had someone put them in their place and because of my own sense of humour, they may think I am their grandfather and decided it would be safer to move on.

Kate and friend in
head dress

Kate and friend

Kate with Gurkha Malaysian friends

Kate with the Gurkha Pipers

Kate with friends

LAST MAN STANDING

After dinner that evening, which we had in the bistro once more, we returned to the Regency Club to make plans for tomorrow. We thought a trip to some of our old locations where there had been some sort of incident or action. This would entail using the old roads. Next morning, I asked Joe to call Silver to meet us at the front of the Regency Club at 09.30 and right on time he was there and ready to roll.

And that was exactly what we did and we headed for Sunga Lembing. This is where my friend Bill and me were billeted with Mr & Mrs Black all those years ago. The tin mine is long gone, but there is a small museum and a picture gallery in which there were some pictures of the very kind couple, who will always have a place in my heart and I assure you Bill felt as I did.

Then it was time to move on. Next stop Bentong. This is where I recall the time that we had a somewhat messy engagement, which involved crossing a not very wide sungon (river). But though it was not wide, the river was in flood. It was the end of the monsoon season. I recall how I'd been rather concerned as I could not swim, but it was Bill to the rescue. He was a powerful swimmer and he would secure a line on the opposite bank. This enabled the full troop to cross as we took four of the CT's out of circulation with no loss to us. On this visit, I found the very spot where it all took place. They have constructed a rather nice wooden bridge. It is now part of a park, so it would appear to have arrived too late to cross the river in comfort. One mustn't complain, for at the least I had the opportunity when some others didn't.

If at times I sound rather bitter regarding some of the things we had to endure, I can assure the reader I am not alone in my feelings. But I will try to express and address this at the end, for others who served in this tiring, strength sapping and protracted campaign. Meanwhile, returning to my granddaughter and our tour of areas, in what I now call my mis-spent youth. Some may ask, does she really want to do this? I think the answer would be yes, for this is not just my history it is our family's history. Kate is an extremely intelligent young lady, very bright and beautiful and to me she also has lots of her Grandma Betty's ways. I don't get a lot of chances to see her as she works away from home and therefore it's a delight to have her accompany me on this, most probably my final trip to this wonderful land and my much-appreciated Malayan friends.

For the record we arrived back at the hotel in time for dinner. As we dined that evening in the bistro my good friend Matty the chef came and sat with us. I naturally thanked him for taking such good care of both myself and Kate. He said it was an honour and privilege to cater and serve us and he would be preparing something special of us on our last evening. I had informed him that we would be away for the next two nights, but he was expecting that, as he knew I always went to Gods Little Acre at Batu Gajah. This is where most of our comrades who fell in the conflict were buried. Silver

would take us there and we would all stay at
Ipoh overnight. Whilst there Kate and I would
be laying two wreaths at the Gurkhas Cemetery
in what is now known as Tambun Road Camp, but
I always think of it as Regimental HQ. After
the service there was a buffet reception at the
Royal Ipoh Club. The wreaths that Kate and I
laid were on behalf of Joanna Lumley and Sir
Garry Johnson KCB OBE MC.

We left Ipoh at about 1:00pm to return to
Kuantan arriving about 7:00pm. A quick shower,
then up to the bistro for dinner and along to
the club for Kate to meet her new friends, and
I would meet a Tiger or two. And so, to bed
to be prepared to greet another day as it was
almost time to go home.

Kate and I decided we would have a quiet
and restful day by the pool for this would be our
last chance before heading home. I advised Kate
to send her laundry to be washed and ironed,
as I was sending my own and they should have
it back in your room by 3:00pm. Then you only
need to keep out what you will be travelling
in. The beauty of this, no big pile of washing
when you arrive home.

This taken care of and it's chill-out
time. Lounger down, umbrella up, ice bucket
filled and three bottles of Tiger (paradise).
My dream was disturbed by a visit from Matty
the chef. He apologised for disturbing me for
which there was no need, but he had come to
let me know I did not have to stick rigidly
to the bistro menu. Whatever I would like, he
would cook it himself. I suggested, "how about

a mixed grill and for Kate an exotic tropical dessert?" As I expected, dinner that evening for us was a pure delight. Matty had truly excelled himself.

This was followed by a stroll about the hotel, saying our goodbyes to our rooms and lay out our travel clothing for tomorrow cup of tea and off to bed with that long journey ahead of us. I Love You Malaysia.

I arose at 6:00am, had a cup of tea, showered, dressed and then went for breakfast. I found that Kate was already there. Fazea was sitting at Kate's table talking to her. She began to get up and I told her to stay, as I was going to get some breakfast. When I got some toast and spread, I sat with them. Fazea advised me that she had spoken to Silver, and he would drive round to the club to pick us up. As we were having our meal, Silver collected our luggage and loaded the car. Then it was time for teardrops and hugging. Joe had come along from reception to see us off. I know what was in my mind and I am sure it was in theirs, that we would never meet again. Very emotional and very sad.

In what was my present mindset, I just wanted to get home. There is little more I can say, a routine flight, long boring, nothing remarkable and just glad to be home at the end of it.

Within a week I attended my last reunion and AGM, where I retired from national office. I then slid into retirement to spend time with my

LAST MAN STANDING

family and friends, celebrate my 90th birthday and start to write this book.

THE END

*(**Not quite**: David is still with us, as he would say 'waiting in the departure lounge'. In the words of Peter Pan 'to die would be an awfully big adventure'. David, thank you for the many interesting hours typing up your memoires it has been a pleasure and an honour. Valerie Nisbet [Editor])*

CHAPTER 15

Winners & Losers

I am sure that there are not a great number of people who would want to go to war. This may come as a surprise to some who don't see me in that warrior roll, because I went off and enrolled in the army. I suppose in a perverse way I was escaping from a form of tyranny that was closer to home. Possibly the second-best thing I ever did.

Oh yes for the more curious the first thing was falling in love at the right place and time with the right girl.

As for soldiering, I can safely say it changed my life. I became more confident and assertive; one or two adjustments and the only way is up.

I have indicated several times in this book that I would write a short, but I hope meaningful article on something which has disturbed me for many years. This matter has really got under my skin and so, I will begin.

To illuminate this subject further in an attempt to clarify my sorrow and for a number of reasons disgust, at the blatant disregard of any form of respect for the service personnel who served and those who gave their lives in what is always referred to as the Malayan Emergency 1948-1960. "My God!" Some would say, "That was a hell of an emergency." Twelve bloody years and when I say bloody, I am being graphic. A completely misguided and thoughtless title for this campaign. The very name leaves one to ponder, for it may confuse someone who knows little or nothing of this conflict. No doubt that was the purpose of the exercise, a smoke screen and a touch of the Fawlty Towers (Don't mention the war).

I will attempt to elaborate. In 1947 the communists predominantly from the Chinese so called immigrant population, launched a series of attacks on British interests such as tree slashing on rubber estates or causing disruption or damage on British owned tin mines. This continued through into 1948 and the culmination came with the murder of two British estate managers on the 18th June, which appears to have been the signal for all-out war. This is where I wish to make my point, for this is when the enemy began to emerge from their jungle hide-outs and a war had begun. Oops sorry, slip of the tongue. I must have been incorrect for the government said, "no silly boy, it's just an emergency. It's only a police action." The purpose for this totally inaccurate statement was to create what would be a political fog, for financial reasons and to keep the planters and tin miners on side. For these were our biggest dollar earners. Therefore, if they were to call it an emergency the insurance companies would pay out for damages to their stock and property, but in a war would not.

We have been told it is too late now to do anything about it. I hope some of the readers will be asking, who is he referring to? That would be our government. Or to be more accurate, successive British governments since 1948 and that is regardless of political party. We even had to fight to be permitted the Malaysian Awarded Medal the PJM. But that was only to those who served after 1957. Those who were engaged in the period 1948 to 1957 were deemed ineligible. The truly sickening fact about this, is that anyone who knew about this campaign is aware the combat was unrelenting and a look at the records of that time show the number of causalities at its height.

To conclude, this my own very personal view of those long-gone days. Lodged in my mind, are those who never returned. Particularly the boys doing their National Service who were most of those KIA. God Bless. For the record, I was a Regular (no complaint).

Picture Credits

Many of the pictures included in the book are from the authors person collection.

A note on the author

I am not a writer of stories and freely admit at not being prolific in putting pen to paper. But I have undertaken this endeavour to, as I'll put it, appease my family and friends. It tells about my life and the experiences of my 90+ years.

I served in khaki uniform for twenty of those years, almost four of them in the Malaysian Emergency. During this time, I was ambushed three times and on one occasion left with life threatening injuries, having to be air lifted to BMH Singapore where he was a patient for 13 weeks, before being returned to action with his very special unit.

It must be understood this is not a diary but more a chronicle of events which had either an elevating or depressing effect on my everyday life.

I guess it also reveals me as a rather unashamed romantic, which I'll proudly admit, but I was never a flirt.

A note on the typeface

The text of this book is set in Nimbus Mono.
The type was invented in 1984 by URW Foundry
GmbH in Hamburg, Germany, and is one of the
Ghostscript family of fonts. The type shares
many visual features with the font Courier,
but with a more bold presence on the page and
a cleaner, more legible aesthetic for ease of
reading.

Glossary

1,2,3...
2 I/C   Second in Command
252   Army Charge Sheet

A
AFV   Armoured Fighting Vehicle
AGM   Annual General Meeting
APC   Armoured Personnel Carrier
ATS   Auxiliary Territorial Service
B
BMH   British Military Hospital

C
CIV   Command Inspection Vehicles
CO   Commanding Officer
CT   Communist Terrorist

G
GHQ   General Headquarters
GPMG   General Purpose Machine Gun
Guidon   Flag
Gurkha   Nepalese Soldier, part of to the
           British Army
H
HQ   Headquarters

I
ID   Identification

J
JWS   Jungle Warfare School

K
Kampong   Village

LAST MAN STANDING

KIA	Killed in Action
KL	Kuala Lumpur

L

LAD	Light Aide Detachment

M

MC	Master of Ceremony
MOD	Ministry of Defence
MP	Member of Parliament

N

NAAFI	Navy, Army & Air-force Institutes
NCO	None Commissioned Officer
NEC	National Executive Committee
NMBVA	National Malaya & Borneo Veterans Association

O

OCPD	Officer Commanding Police District
OG	Orders Group
OP	Observation Post

P

PC	Police Constable
PE	Physical Exercise
PJM	Pingat Jasa Malaysia Medal
PSI	Permanent Staff Instructor
PTC	Primary Training Centre
PTI	Physical Training Instructor
PWD	Public Works Department

Q

QARANC	Queen Alexandra's Royal Army Nursing Corps
QM	Quartermaster

R

RAC	Royal Armoured Corps
RASC	Royal Army Service Corps
REME	Royal Electrical & Mechanical Engineers
RHQ	Regimental Headquarters
ROS	Regimental Orderly Sergeant
RP	Regimental Police
RSM	Regimental Sergeant Major
RTO	Rail Transport Office
RTU	Return to Unit

S

Siam	Now Thailand
SL	Squadron Leader
SSM	Squadron Sergeant Major
Sungei	River

T

TA	Territorial Army
TAVR	Territorial & Army Volunteer Reserve

LAST MAN STANDING

Acknowledgements

Sir Garry Johnson KCB, OBE, MC
Colonel Tony Gibson
David M Neil
All the Neil Family
Rev'd Timothy Duff
Mr Cyril Goodhand
Mrs Brenda Dudding
Mrs Sharon McGonagal
Mark Fairley
Valerie Nisbet

The author would like to extend his humblest thanks to all of the aforementioned, without whom this project would not have been possible.

A Tribute to Val the Editor.

It is time to give thanks and praise to the one person who has been so important in the writing of this book. I know she has spent many long hours transcribing my longhand into legible print, which I consider amazing. I hear someone say, "that's not amazing, anyone can do that." A very sweeping statement for someone to make and if I knew who made it, I would challenge him or her to a wager and would win handsomely. For whoever they maybe they would have lost before they start, as her secret is to have the ability to transcribe *my longhand* (no contest).

DAVID NEIL

And now for the real Val.

Let me begin by my own assessment. She is
diligent, extremely capable and undoubtedly
efficient to the point of at times making me
feel surplus to requirement. I only said that
for if I did not, she would think I didn't like
her anymore. But all joking aside, I could not
have a brighter or more efficient assistant in
writing not only this book, but she was onboard
with the three poetry books **wot I have written**.
It will feel strange not conferring with her
on a day to day basis. If the book should fail,
it would be no reflection on Val. Her input was
honest and true.

The Last Salute

By Dave Neil

If this book you chose to read
It tells of men, a special breed
Who battled in a jungle hell
Sad to say, some of them fell

This book I wish to dedicate
Among those fallen was my mate
They could not stop to say goodbye
But let me tell you, soldiers cry